Mometrix

TEST PREPARATION

Common Core Grade 6 English Language Arts Secrets Study Guide

I07B6926

DEAR FUTURE EXAM SUCCESS STORY

First of all, **THANK YOU** for purchasing Mometrix study materials!

Second, congratulations! You are one of the few determined test-takers who are committed to doing whatever it takes to excel on your exam. **You have come to the right place.** We developed these study materials with one goal in mind: to deliver you the information you need in a format that's concise and easy to use.

In addition to optimizing your guide for the content of the test, we've outlined our recommended steps for breaking down the preparation process into small, attainable goals so you can make sure you stay on track.

We've also analyzed the entire test-taking process, identifying the most common pitfalls and showing how you can overcome them and be ready for any curveball the test throws you.

Standardized testing is one of the biggest obstacles on your road to success, which only increases the importance of doing well in the high-pressure, high-stakes environment of test day. Your results on this test could have a significant impact on your future, and this guide provides the information and practical advice to help you achieve your full potential on test day.

Your success is our success

We would love to hear from you! If you would like to share the story of your exam success or if you have any questions or comments in regard to our products, please contact us at **800-673-8175** or **support@mometrix.com**.

Thanks again for your business and we wish you continued success!

Sincerely,
The Mometrix Test Preparation Team

Need more help? Check out our flashcards at:
http://MometrixFlashcards.com/CCSS

Written and edited by the Mometrix Exam Secrets Test Prep Team
Printed in the United States of America

Table of Contents

Introduction

Thank you for purchasing this resource! You have made the choice to prepare yourself for a test that could have a huge impact on your future, and this guide is designed to help you be fully ready for test day. Obviously, it's important to have a solid understanding of the test material, but you also need to be prepared for the unique environment and stressors of the test, so that you can perform to the best of your abilities.

For this purpose, the first section that appears in this guide is the **Secret Keys**. We've devoted countless hours to meticulously researching what works and what doesn't, and we've boiled down our findings to the five most impactful steps you can take to improve your performance on the test. We start at the beginning with study planning and move through the preparation process, all the way to the testing strategies that will help you get the most out of what you know when you're finally sitting in front of the test.

We recommend that you start preparing for your test as far in advance as possible. However, if you've bought this guide as a last-minute study resource and only have a few days before your test, we recommend that you skip over the first two Secret Keys since they address a long-term study plan.

If you struggle with **test anxiety**, we strongly encourage you to check out our recommendations for how you can overcome it. Test anxiety is a formidable foe, but it can be beaten, and we want to make sure you have the tools you need to defeat it.

Secret Key #1 – Plan Big, Study Small

There's a lot riding on your performance. If you want to ace this test, you're going to need to keep your skills sharp and the material fresh in your mind. You need a plan that lets you review everything you need to know while still fitting in your schedule. We'll break this strategy down into three categories.

Information Organization

Start with the information you already have: the official test outline. From this, you can make a complete list of all the concepts you need to cover before the test. Organize these concepts into groups that can be studied together, and create a list of any related vocabulary you need to learn so you can brush up on any difficult terms. You'll want to keep this vocabulary list handy once you actually start studying since you may need to add to it along the way.

Time Management

Once you have your set of study concepts, decide how to spread them out over the time you have left before the test. Break your study plan into small, clear goals so you have a manageable task for each day and know exactly what you're doing. Then just focus on one small step at a time. When you manage your time this way, you don't need to spend hours at a time studying. Studying a small block of content for a short period each day helps you retain information better and avoid stressing over how much you have left to do. You can relax knowing that you have a plan to cover everything in time. In order for this strategy to be effective though, you have to start studying early and stick to your schedule. Avoid the exhaustion and futility that comes from last-minute cramming!

Study Environment

The environment you study in has a big impact on your learning. Studying in a coffee shop, while probably more enjoyable, is not likely to be as fruitful as studying in a quiet room. It's important to keep distractions to a minimum. You're only planning to study for a short block of time, so make the most of it. Don't pause to check your phone or get up to find a snack. It's also important to **avoid multitasking**. Research has consistently shown that multitasking will make your studying dramatically less effective. Your study area should also be comfortable and well-lit so you don't have the distraction of straining your eyes or sitting on an uncomfortable chair.

The time of day you study is also important. You want to be rested and alert. Don't wait until just before bedtime. Study when you'll be most likely to comprehend and remember. Even better, if you know what time of day your test will be, set that time aside for study. That way your brain will be used to working on that subject at that specific time and you'll have a better chance of recalling information.

Finally, it can be helpful to team up with others who are studying for the same test. Your actual studying should be done in as isolated an environment as possible, but the work of organizing the information and setting up the study plan can be divided up. In between study sessions, you can discuss with your teammates the concepts that you're all studying and quiz each other on the details. Just be sure that your teammates are as serious about the test as you are. If you find that your study time is being replaced with social time, you might need to find a new team.

Secret Key #2 – Make Your Studying Count

You're devoting a lot of time and effort to preparing for this test, so you want to be absolutely certain it will pay off. This means doing more than just reading the content and hoping you can remember it on test day. It's important to make every minute of study count. There are two main areas you can focus on to make your studying count.

Retention

It doesn't matter how much time you study if you can't remember the material. You need to make sure you are retaining the concepts. To check your retention of the information you're learning, try recalling it at later times with minimal prompting. Try carrying around flashcards and glance at one or two from time to time or ask a friend who's also studying for the test to quiz you.

To enhance your retention, look for ways to put the information into practice so that you can apply it rather than simply recalling it. If you're using the information in practical ways, it will be much easier to remember. Similarly, it helps to solidify a concept in your mind if you're not only reading it to yourself but also explaining it to someone else. Ask a friend to let you teach them about a concept you're a little shaky on (or speak aloud to an imaginary audience if necessary). As you try to summarize, define, give examples, and answer your friend's questions, you'll understand the concepts better and they will stay with you longer. Finally, step back for a big picture view and ask yourself how each piece of information fits with the whole subject. When you link the different concepts together and see them working together as a whole, it's easier to remember the individual components.

Finally, practice showing your work on any multi-step problems, even if you're just studying. Writing out each step you take to solve a problem will help solidify the process in your mind, and you'll be more likely to remember it during the test.

Modality

Modality simply refers to the means or method by which you study. Choosing a study modality that fits your own individual learning style is crucial. No two people learn best in exactly the same way, so it's important to know your strengths and use them to your advantage.

For example, if you learn best by visualization, focus on visualizing a concept in your mind and draw an image or a diagram. Try color-coding your notes, illustrating them, or creating symbols that will trigger your mind to recall a learned concept. If you learn best by hearing or discussing information, find a study partner who learns the same way or read aloud to yourself. Think about how to put the information in your own words. Imagine that you are giving a lecture on the topic and record yourself so you can listen to it later.

For any learning style, flashcards can be helpful. Organize the information so you can take advantage of spare moments to review. Underline key words or phrases. Use different colors for different categories. Mnemonic devices (such as creating a short list in which every item starts with the same letter) can also help with retention. Find what works best for you and use it to store the information in your mind most effectively and easily.

Secret Key #3 – Practice the Right Way

Your success on test day depends not only on how many hours you put into preparing, but also on whether you prepared the right way. It's good to check along the way to see if your studying is paying off. One of the most effective ways to do this is by taking practice tests to evaluate your progress. Practice tests are useful because they show exactly where you need to improve. Every time you take a practice test, pay special attention to these three groups of questions:

- The questions you got wrong
- The questions you had to guess on, even if you guessed right
- The questions you found difficult or slow to work through

This will show you exactly what your weak areas are, and where you need to devote more study time. Ask yourself why each of these questions gave you trouble. Was it because you didn't understand the material? Was it because you didn't remember the vocabulary? Do you need more repetitions on this type of question to build speed and confidence? Dig into those questions and figure out how you can strengthen your weak areas as you go back to review the material.

Additionally, many practice tests have a section explaining the answer choices. It can be tempting to read the explanation and think that you now have a good understanding of the concept. However, an explanation likely only covers part of the question's broader context. Even if the explanation makes perfect sense, **go back and investigate** every concept related to the question until you're positive you have a thorough understanding.

As you go along, keep in mind that the practice test is just that: practice. Memorizing these questions and answers will not be very helpful on the actual test because it is unlikely to have any of the same exact questions. If you only know the right answers to the sample questions, you won't be prepared for the real thing. **Study the concepts** until you understand them fully, and then you'll be able to answer any question that shows up on the test.

It's important to wait on the practice tests until you're ready. If you take a test on your first day of study, you may be overwhelmed by the amount of material covered and how much you need to learn. Work up to it gradually.

On test day, you'll need to be prepared for answering questions, managing your time, and using the test-taking strategies you've learned. It's a lot to balance, like a mental marathon that will have a big impact on your future. Like training for a marathon, you'll need to start slowly and work your way up. When test day arrives, you'll be ready.

Start with the strategies you've read in the first two Secret Keys—plan your course and study in the way that works best for you. If you have time, consider using multiple study resources to get different approaches to the same concepts. It can be helpful to see difficult concepts from more than one angle. Then find a good source for practice tests. Many times, the test website will suggest potential study resources or provide sample tests.

Practice Test Strategy

If you're able to find at least three practice tests, we recommend this strategy:

Untimed and Open-Book Practice

Take the first test with no time constraints and with your notes and study guide handy. Take your time and focus on applying the strategies you've learned.

Timed and Open-Book Practice

Take the second practice test open-book as well, but set a timer and practice pacing yourself to finish in time.

Timed and Closed-Book Practice

Take any other practice tests as if it were test day. Set a timer and put away your study materials. Sit at a table or desk in a quiet room, imagine yourself at the testing center, and answer questions as quickly and accurately as possible.

Keep repeating timed and closed-book tests on a regular basis until you run out of practice tests or it's time for the actual test. Your mind will be ready for the schedule and stress of test day, and you'll be able to focus on recalling the material you've learned.

Secret Key #4 – Pace Yourself

Once you're fully prepared for the material on the test, your biggest challenge on test day will be managing your time. Just knowing that the clock is ticking can make you panic even if you have plenty of time left. Work on pacing yourself so you can build confidence against the time constraints of the exam. Pacing is a difficult skill to master, especially in a high-pressure environment, so **practice is vital**.

Set time expectations for your pace based on how much time is available. For example, if a section has 60 questions and the time limit is 30 minutes, you know you have to average 30 seconds or less per question in order to answer them all. Although 30 seconds is the hard limit, set 25 seconds per question as your goal, so you reserve extra time to spend on harder questions. When you budget extra time for the harder questions, you no longer have any reason to stress when those questions take longer to answer.

Don't let this time expectation distract you from working through the test at a calm, steady pace, but keep it in mind so you don't spend too much time on any one question. Recognize that taking extra time on one question you don't understand may keep you from answering two that you do understand later in the test. If your time limit for a question is up and you're still not sure of the answer, mark it and move on, and come back to it later if the time and the test format allow. If the testing format doesn't allow you to return to earlier questions, just make an educated guess; then put it out of your mind and move on.

On the easier questions, be careful not to rush. It may seem wise to hurry through them so you have more time for the challenging ones, but it's not worth missing one if you know the concept and just didn't take the time to read the question fully. Work efficiently but make sure you understand the question and have looked at all of the answer choices, since more than one may seem right at first.

Even if you're paying attention to the time, you may find yourself a little behind at some point. You should speed up to get back on track, but do so wisely. Don't panic; just take a few seconds less on each question until you're caught up. Don't guess without thinking, but do look through the answer choices and eliminate any you know are wrong. If you can get down to two choices, it is often worthwhile to guess from those. Once you've chosen an answer, move on and don't dwell on any that you skipped or had to hurry through. If a question was taking too long, chances are it was one of the harder ones, so you weren't as likely to get it right anyway.

On the other hand, if you find yourself getting ahead of schedule, it may be beneficial to slow down a little. The more quickly you work, the more likely you are to make a careless mistake that will affect your score. You've budgeted time for each question, so don't be afraid to spend that time. Practice an efficient but careful pace to get the most out of the time you have.

Secret Key #5 – Have a Plan for Guessing

When you're taking the test, you may find yourself stuck on a question. Some of the answer choices seem better than others, but you don't see the one answer choice that is obviously correct. What do you do?

The scenario described above is very common, yet most test takers have not effectively prepared for it. Developing and practicing a plan for guessing may be one of the single most effective uses of your time as you get ready for the exam.

In developing your plan for guessing, there are three questions to address:

- When should you start the guessing process?
- How should you narrow down the choices?
- Which answer should you choose?

When to Start the Guessing Process

Unless your plan for guessing is to select C every time (which, despite its merits, is not what we recommend), you need to leave yourself enough time to apply your answer elimination strategies. Since you have a limited amount of time for each question, that means that if you're going to give yourself the best shot at guessing correctly, you have to decide quickly whether or not you will guess.

Of course, the best-case scenario is that you don't have to guess at all, so first, see if you can answer the question based on your knowledge of the subject and basic reasoning skills. Focus on the key words in the question and try to jog your memory of related topics. Give yourself a chance to bring the knowledge to mind, but once you realize that you don't have (or you can't access) the knowledge you need to answer the question, it's time to start the guessing process.

It's almost always better to start the guessing process too early than too late. It only takes a few seconds to remember something and answer the question from knowledge. Carefully eliminating wrong answer choices takes longer. Plus, going through the process of eliminating answer choices can actually help jog your memory.

Summary: Start the guessing process as soon as you decide that you can't answer the question based on your knowledge.

How to Narrow Down the Choices

The next chapter in this book (**Test-Taking Strategies**) includes a wide range of strategies for how to approach questions and how to look for answer choices to eliminate. You will definitely want to read those carefully, practice them, and figure out which ones work best for you. Here though, we're going to address a mindset rather than a particular strategy.

Your odds of guessing an answer correctly depend on how many options you are choosing from.

Number of options left	5	4	3	2	1
Odds of guessing correctly	20%	25%	33%	50%	100%

You can see from this chart just how valuable it is to be able to eliminate incorrect answers and make an educated guess, but there are two things that many test takers do that cause them to miss out on the benefits of guessing:

- Accidentally eliminating the correct answer
- Selecting an answer based on an impression

We'll look at the first one here, and the second one in the next section.

To avoid accidentally eliminating the correct answer, we recommend a thought exercise called **the $5 challenge**. In this challenge, you only eliminate an answer choice from contention if you are willing to bet $5 on it being wrong. Why $5? Five dollars is a small but not insignificant amount of money. It's an amount you could afford to lose but wouldn't want to throw away. And while losing $5 once might not hurt too much, doing it twenty times will set you back $100. In the same way, each small decision you make—eliminating a choice here, guessing on a question there—won't by itself impact your score very much, but when you put them all together, they can make a big difference. By holding each answer choice elimination decision to a higher standard, you can reduce the risk of accidentally eliminating the correct answer.

The $5 challenge can also be applied in a positive sense: If you are willing to bet $5 that an answer choice *is* correct, go ahead and mark it as correct.

Summary: Only eliminate an answer choice if you are willing to bet $5 that it is wrong.

Which Answer to Choose

You're taking the test. You've run into a hard question and decided you'll have to guess. You've eliminated all the answer choices you're willing to bet $5 on. Now you have to pick an answer. Why do we even need to talk about this? Why can't you just pick whichever one you feel like when the time comes?

The answer to these questions is that if you don't come into the test with a plan, you'll rely on your impression to select an answer choice, and if you do that, you risk falling into a trap. The test writers know that everyone who takes their test will be guessing on some of the questions, so they intentionally write wrong answer choices to seem plausible. You still have to pick an answer though, and if the wrong answer choices are designed to look right, how can you ever be sure that you're not falling for their trap? The best solution we've found to this dilemma is to take the decision out of your hands entirely. Here is the process we recommend:

Once you've eliminated any choices that you are confident (willing to bet $5) are wrong, select the first remaining choice as your answer.

Whether you choose to select the first remaining choice, the second, or the last, the important thing is that you use some preselected standard. Using this approach guarantees that you will not be enticed into selecting an answer choice that looks right, because you are not basing your decision on how the answer choices look.

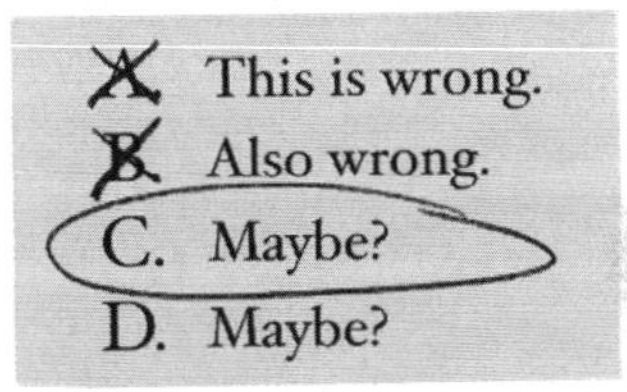

This is not meant to make you question your knowledge. Instead, it is to help you recognize the difference between your knowledge and your impressions. There's a huge difference between thinking an answer is right because of what you know, and thinking an answer is right because it looks or sounds like it should be right.

Summary: To ensure that your selection is appropriately random, make a predetermined selection from among all answer choices you have not eliminated.

Test-Taking Strategies

This section contains a list of test-taking strategies that you may find helpful as you work through the test. By taking what you know and applying logical thought, you can maximize your chances of answering any question correctly!

It is very important to realize that every question is different and every person is different: no single strategy will work on every question, and no single strategy will work for every person. That's why we've included all of them here, so you can try them out and determine which ones work best for different types of questions and which ones work best for you.

Question Strategies

✓ Read Carefully

Read the question and the answer choices carefully. Don't miss the question because you misread the terms. You have plenty of time to read each question thoroughly and make sure you understand what is being asked. Yet a happy medium must be attained, so don't waste too much time. You must read carefully and efficiently.

✓ Contextual Clues

Look for contextual clues. If the question includes a word you are not familiar with, look at the immediate context for some indication of what the word might mean. Contextual clues can often give you all the information you need to decipher the meaning of an unfamiliar word. Even if you can't determine the meaning, you may be able to narrow down the possibilities enough to make a solid guess at the answer to the question.

✓ Prefixes

If you're having trouble with a word in the question or answer choices, try dissecting it. Take advantage of every clue that the word might include. Prefixes can be a huge help. Usually, they allow you to determine a basic meaning. *Pre-* means before, *post-* means after, *pro-* is positive, *de-* is negative. From prefixes, you can get an idea of the general meaning of the word and try to put it into context.

✓ Hedge Words

Watch out for critical hedge words, such as *likely, may, can, often, almost, mostly, usually, generally, rarely,* and *sometimes.* Question writers insert these hedge phrases to cover every possibility. Often an answer choice will be wrong simply because it leaves no room for exception. Be on guard for answer choices that have definitive words such as *exactly* and *always.*

✓ Switchback Words

Stay alert for *switchbacks.* These are the words and phrases frequently used to alert you to shifts in thought. The most common switchback words are *but, although,* and *however.* Others include *nevertheless, on the other hand, even though, while, in spite of, despite,* and *regardless of.* Switchback words are important to catch because they can change the direction of the question or an answer choice.

☑ Face Value

When in doubt, use common sense. Accept the situation in the problem at face value. Don't read too much into it. These problems will not require you to make wild assumptions. If you have to go beyond creativity and warp time or space in order to have an answer choice fit the question, then you should move on and consider the other answer choices. These are normal problems rooted in reality. The applicable relationship or explanation may not be readily apparent, but it is there for you to figure out. Use your common sense to interpret anything that isn't clear.

Answer Choice Strategies

☑ Answer Selection

The most thorough way to pick an answer choice is to identify and eliminate wrong answers until only one is left, then confirm it is the correct answer. Sometimes an answer choice may immediately seem right, but be careful. The test writers will usually put more than one reasonable answer choice on each question, so take a second to read all of them and make sure that the other choices are not equally obvious. As long as you have time left, it is better to read every answer choice than to pick the first one that looks right without checking the others.

☑ Answer Choice Families

An answer choice family consists of two (in rare cases, three) answer choices that are very similar in construction and cannot all be true at the same time. If you see two answer choices that are direct opposites or parallels, one of them is usually the correct answer. For instance, if one answer choice says that quantity *x* increases and another either says that quantity *x* decreases (opposite) or says that quantity *y* increases (parallel), then those answer choices would fall into the same family. An answer choice that doesn't match the construction of the answer choice family is more likely to be incorrect. Most questions will not have answer choice families, but when they do appear, you should be prepared to recognize them.

☑ Eliminate Answers

Eliminate answer choices as soon as you realize they are wrong, but make sure you consider all possibilities. If you are eliminating answer choices and realize that the last one you are left with is also wrong, don't panic. Start over and consider each choice again. There may be something you missed the first time that you will realize on the second pass.

☑ Avoid Fact Traps

Don't be distracted by an answer choice that is factually true but doesn't answer the question. You are looking for the choice that answers the question. Stay focused on what the question is asking for so you don't accidentally pick an answer that is true but incorrect. Always go back to the question and make sure the answer choice you've selected actually answers the question and is not merely a true statement.

☑ Extreme Statements

In general, you should avoid answers that put forth extreme actions as standard practice or proclaim controversial ideas as established fact. An answer choice that states the "process should be used in certain situations, if…" is much more likely to be correct than one that states the "process should be discontinued completely." The first is a calm rational statement and doesn't even make a definitive, uncompromising stance, using a hedge word *if* to provide wiggle room, whereas the second choice is far more extreme.

⊘ BENCHMARK

As you read through the answer choices and you come across one that seems to answer the question well, mentally select that answer choice. This is not your final answer, but it's the one that will help you evaluate the other answer choices. The one that you selected is your benchmark or standard for judging each of the other answer choices. Every other answer choice must be compared to your benchmark. That choice is correct until proven otherwise by another answer choice beating it. If you find a better answer, then that one becomes your new benchmark. Once you've decided that no other choice answers the question as well as your benchmark, you have your final answer.

⊘ PREDICT THE ANSWER

Before you even start looking at the answer choices, it is often best to try to predict the answer. When you come up with the answer on your own, it is easier to avoid distractions and traps because you will know exactly what to look for. The right answer choice is unlikely to be word-for-word what you came up with, but it should be a close match. Even if you are confident that you have the right answer, you should still take the time to read each option before moving on.

General Strategies

⊘ TOUGH QUESTIONS

If you are stumped on a problem or it appears too hard or too difficult, don't waste time. Move on! Remember though, if you can quickly check for obviously incorrect answer choices, your chances of guessing correctly are greatly improved. Before you completely give up, at least try to knock out a couple of possible answers. Eliminate what you can and then guess at the remaining answer choices before moving on.

⊘ CHECK YOUR WORK

Since you will probably not know every term listed and the answer to every question, it is important that you get credit for the ones that you do know. Don't miss any questions through careless mistakes. If at all possible, try to take a second to look back over your answer selection and make sure you've selected the correct answer choice and haven't made a costly careless mistake (such as marking an answer choice that you didn't mean to mark). This quick double check should more than pay for itself in caught mistakes for the time it costs.

⊘ PACE YOURSELF

It's easy to be overwhelmed when you're looking at a page full of questions; your mind is confused and full of random thoughts, and the clock is ticking down faster than you would like. Calm down and maintain the pace that you have set for yourself. Especially as you get down to the last few minutes of the test, don't let the small numbers on the clock make you panic. As long as you are on track by monitoring your pace, you are guaranteed to have time for each question.

⊘ DON'T RUSH

It is very easy to make errors when you are in a hurry. Maintaining a fast pace in answering questions is pointless if it makes you miss questions that you would have gotten right otherwise. Test writers like to include distracting information and wrong answers that seem right. Taking a little extra time to avoid careless mistakes can make all the difference in your test score. Find a pace that allows you to be confident in the answers that you select.

✅ Keep Moving

Panicking will not help you pass the test, so do your best to stay calm and keep moving. Taking deep breaths and going through the answer elimination steps you practiced can help to break through a stress barrier and keep your pace.

Final Notes

The combination of a solid foundation of content knowledge and the confidence that comes from practicing your plan for applying that knowledge is the key to maximizing your performance on test day. As your foundation of content knowledge is built up and strengthened, you'll find that the strategies included in this chapter become more and more effective in helping you quickly sift through the distractions and traps of the test to isolate the correct answer.

Now that you're preparing to move forward into the test content chapters of this book, be sure to keep your goal in mind. As you read, think about how you will be able to apply this information on the test. If you've already seen sample questions for the test and you have an idea of the question format and style, try to come up with questions of your own that you can answer based on what you're reading. This will give you valuable practice applying your knowledge in the same ways you can expect to on test day.

Good luck and good studying!

Reading

Literature

Explicit Information

Explicit information is the term for information that is directly stated in a story or passage. It is what the author tells you. It is not information that is hinted at or that you have to make a conclusion about. Explicit information can be facts or details about an event, something or someone. There is usually a lot of explicit information in a story and this information is often used to make an inference or draw a conclusion. To answer questions that ask about explicit information, simply reread the story until you find the answer. In fiction, details about characters, events, and setting are often explicit.

Read the following excerpt and tell what information is explicit.

> From his bed, Steve could see the moon begin to rise and the stars twinkle. He could hear the nurses as they walked down the long hall, their footsteps echoing in the quiet.

The explicit information in the excerpt is all about Steve and what he could see and hear. The passage says that he could see the moon begin to rise and the stars twinkle from his bed. It also says that he could hear the nurses walking down the hall. This is explicit information. The author is describing what Steve can see and hear. There is nothing that is hinted at in the excerpt except that Steve seems to be in a hospital. However, that conclusion is not explicit information. The author does not say this directly, so it is implicit information.

Inference

An *inference* is what a reader can deduce from the information in a passage. It is what the story may hint about, and what a reader can conclude as a result of what the author says in the passage. It is also the best guess that a reader can make based on what happened or was said or in a story. A good inference is based on or supported by details in the passage. For instance, if a passage says that Joan is holding her mouth and moaning, you might conclude, or *infer*, that she has a sore mouth or a toothache. You cannot be sure of this, but it is the best conclusion that you can reach using the information at hand. Inferences are considered implicit information. They are not found directly in a passage.

Read the following excerpt and tell what you can conclude about why Vicki got a cold.

> Hi Nance,
>
> Richard and I went camping last weekend. A bear ate all our food while we were sleeping. And it was cold and rainy the last night. We have both caught colds. Next time we go camping we are going to bring warmer clothes and extra food for the bears.
>
> Love, Vicki

You can conclude that Vicki got a cold because it was cold and rainy on the last night of her camping trip. She also talks about bringing warmer clothes the next time she goes camping, which further suggests that she was cold. However, the fact that a bear ate her food would have little to do with her getting sick, so that is not the reason she got a cold. It is logical to conclude that she got a cold because of the weather and not having warmer clothes. It is the best inference that you can make from the letter. Inferences are the best guesses that a reader can make based on the information in a passage.

Determining the Theme of a Passage

The *theme* of a passage is the message or lesson that a story teaches. It is what the author wants the reader to learn from the passage, and is the main point or moral that the passage carries with it. The theme of a passage may be stated explicitly, as in the case of a fable, but it is usually not stated. The reader has to combine the information in a story and what happens in that story together to figure out the story's theme. As the details of the story unfold, it reveals the theme; the theme is created through the story's development. The events of a story help shape the kind of theme the passage teaches. For instance, as you read, ask yourself if a character is doing something wrong and, if so, ask yourself if the character is punished at the end of a story. All of this combines to give a theme. Most themes are about life, society, or human nature. Themes also help give a passage unity.

Read the following passage and explain why "It is better not to run away" describes the story's theme.

> Ivan made fun of Sasha. So Sasha was scared of him. If he saw Ivan coming, Sasha hid. Then Sasha changed. He stopped hiding from Ivan. If Ivan laughed at him, Sasha laughed right back. He wasn't afraid anymore. Soon, Ivan stopped making fun of Sasha. This made Sasha feel happier.

The theme "It is better not to run away" fits what happens in the story. Sasha is scared of Ivan and hides from him. But then Sasha stops hiding and laughs back at Ivan, and after that he is not afraid anymore. For him it was better not to run away, but to stay and face his fears. In the end Sasha is happier. He solved his problem. This is the theme that the story teaches through the events of the story. Sasha and the reader learn that something good happened when Sasha did not hide or run away. This is the message of this passage. The reader needs to figure out the theme from what happens in a story.

Objective Summary of a Passage

A summary always includes the main idea of a passage and the most important details that are found in a story. It should explain what a story is about and then include the most important events that make a story different. In order to make the summary objective, you must make sure to reflect what the passage is about rather than how you might feel about the story. A summary should be fairly short. It differs from paraphrasing. *Paraphrasing* rewords the main idea but also uses many more details about a story than a summary does. Summaries allow the reader to remember what was most important about a story. Summaries do not include a reader's personal feelings or judgments about the story.

Read the following and explain why it is not a good summary.

> *Cinderella* is the story of a girl. Her step-sisters were mean to her. They wouldn't let her go to the ball. But she went anyway. She met the prince. I love the story of Cinderella. I wish I had a fairy godmother.

This summary includes some of the main idea of the story of Cinderella, that her stepsisters were mean and would not let her go to the ball but that she went anyway and met the prince. However, it leaves out the important information about her having a fairy godmother help her, how she lost her glass slipper, and the fact that the prince finally found and married her. These are all important details not included in the summary. It is also not a good summary because the writer included personal opinions about the story and a desire to have a fairy godmother. A summary should always be objective and not include personal feelings or opinions.

Effect of Plot on a Story's Characters

The *plot* of a story unfolds as each event follows another, shaping the characters as they react to the various events that occur. The plot builds one event at a time and how the characters respond to what happens to them creates not only the plot but also the theme. Some characters are able to resolve their problems by the end of the story, while some characters fail to overcome their predicaments. Characters are revealed in their reactions to the events that take place. Some grow and some do not. It is for the reader to interpret the meaning of the story and understand its characters as they experience the events of a plot.

Read the excerpt and explain how finding the chest affects Marta.

> The map said this was the spot. Marta held her breath. Her fists were clenched into two tight balls. She lifted the shovel and scooped more sand out of the hole. There it was; she had found the chest with the diamonds. She opened the top. She would never need to work again. She smiled. It was really happening.

Marta finds the spot where the chest is. Her fists were clenched into tight balls. She was nervous. But then she saw the chest. She opened it and smiled. She was happy. Finding the chest would change her life. It was filled with diamonds so she would never have to work again. She was happy. This is how the event shaped Marta. It made her happy. Events can cause characters to have all kinds of feelings. Here something wonderful happened. Often, however, events in stories are not quite so happy. For instance, if a robber had suddenly seen Marta and the chest, he might have stolen the chest. Then that event would have had a very different effect on her. Readers need to look for hints about how characters are reacting to events, whether they are simply hinted at or stated in the story. In this way a reader will learn what characters are like.

Determining the Meaning of Words and Phrases as They Are Used in a Text

Readers can use *context clues* to figure out the meaning of unknown words and phrases in a story or passage. The clues may be found in the sentence with the unknown word or phrase in it or in the surrounding sentences. Many words have more than one meaning, so the reader has to examine the context in which a word is used. The word *sink*, for instance, has many meanings. It can mean to invest, to drop or go down, to go to a lower level, to go underwater, to lapse into a condition, to make an impression, and more. So in the sentence, "She was sinking into a coma" the meaning is clearly refers to "sinking" as the act of lapsing into a condition. Phrases must also be understood through context. In the sentence, "Clara felt she was a voice in the wilderness, but time proved her correct," the careful reader can figure out that the expression "voice in the wilderness" means someone expressing an opinion that may be true even if no one believes it.

Read the following sentence and explain how to determine the meaning of the word "unscathed."

> Bill took a bad fall while he was hiking, but when he stood up he found he was unscathed, and went on to finish the hike.

The reader needs to find the context clues in the sentence to figure out the meaning of the word "unscathed." The sentence says that Bill took a bad fall. From this we could conclude that he might have been hurt. But it goes on to say that he was able to finish the hike anyway. So "unscathed" has to mean something like "unhurt." When trying to figure out the meaning of a word, substitute what you feel might be a synonym in place of it and see if it makes sense. In this case, Bill is clearly unhurt by the fall. By doing this you can figure out the correct meaning of unknown words or phrases.

READ THE EXCERPT AND EXPLAIN HOW TO DETERMINE THE MEANING OF "SPREAD LIKE A CANCER."

> At first the army fought bravely, handily repelling the attackers despite being outnumbered almost four to one. But then it was learned that their leader Hector was dead, and fear spread like a cancer from unit to unit, changing what was once a proud and strong organization into a helpless band of stragglers.

The excerpt says that the army fought bravely and repelled attackers even though they were outnumbered. But the effect of hearing that their leader was dead caused fear to "spread like a cancer," causing this once proud army to become a band of stragglers. Certainly the expression "spread like cancer" cannot be a good thing; the reference to the disease also gives the reader a hint of what the expression means. If you substitute "spread very quickly" in place of "spread like a cancer," you will see that it makes sense in the context of the excerpt. This is a way to figure out the meaning of an unknown word or expression.

FIGURATIVE USE OF A WORD OR EXPRESSION

Figurative language is a literary device used by writers to expand reality by creating powerful and vivid images that keep writing fresh and appealing. There are many different kinds of figurative language, including simile, metaphor, personification, and hyperbole. *Similes* compare things using the comparing words "like" or "as." For example, the sentence "Anna is as graceful as a ballerina" uses a simile to describe Anna's grace. *Metaphors* compare things without using comparing words. For example, the sentence "Anna is a ballerina when she dances" uses a metaphor to describe Anna's dancing talent. *Personification* gives human traits to a thing or animal: "The music beckoned Anna to dance" personifies the music, which cannot actually beckon someone because it is not human. Finally, *hyperbole* is an exaggeration that is vivid but not literally believable. Saying that "Anna dances from the moment she wakes up until the moment she goes to sleep" does not really mean that Anna spends her every waking moment dancing; it is a hyperbole that describes how much Anna loves to dance.

READ THE EXCERPT FROM A POEM BY WILLIAM BLAKE AND DESCRIBE WHAT FORM OF FIGURATIVE LANGUAGE IT USES.

The wild winds weep,
And the night is a-cold;
Come hither, sleep,
And my griefs unfold.

The poem is an example of personification. In the poem, the poet says "The wild winds weep," thereby giving the winds the human characteristic of weeping. Later it says "Come hither, sleep," which is another use of personification asking that sleep to go somewhere as though it were a person. The poem gives the winds and sleep human characteristics. This is the definition of personification. It is not an example of simile because there is no comparison using the words "as" or "like." It is not a metaphor because there is no comparison between two things sharing a similar quality. And it is not an example of hyperbole because there is no exaggeration. The poem does contain some alliteration, however; the repetition of the letter "w" in "wild winds weep" qualifies as alliteration, which is another literary technique.

DENOTATIVE VS. CONNOTATIVE MEANING OF WORDS

The *denotative* meaning of a word is what the word means literally. It is the exact dictionary definition of the word. The *connotative* meaning of a word, on the other hand, is what the word suggests. It is the feelings or emotions that the use of the word creates. Words often have associated meanings in addition to their dictionary definition. For example, the word "fragile" is defined in the dictionary as delicate. But another word meaning delicate might be "flimsy," but that word has many other connotations. "Flimsy" has a negative connotation while "fragile" does not. The connotative meaning of a word in a passage can be found by looking at the context clues in the surrounding sentences.

READ THE FOLLOWING SENTENCE AND EXPLAIN THE CONNOTATIVE MEANING OF THE WORD "PALATIAL" AND HOW IT RELATES TO THE WORD "LARGE."

> This house isn't really large, but compared to my apartment it seems palatial.

The words "large" and "palatial" both have the definition meaning of "big." But the word "palatial" means something that is not only big but also very elegant. This word expresses something far beyond just large; it emphasizes how impressive a thing is. The biggest hint to this word's connotations is the fact that it comes from the word "palace." This tells us that it is not just large, but regal as well. Another word that might be similar to "palatial" is "extravagant," but this word has a more negative connotation because it suggests something that is overdone. Words need to be studied for both their denotative and connotative meaning because the connotations that words bring up can flavor a character, setting, or event in a subtle manner.

DEVELOPING THE THEME, SETTING OR PLOT

When a writer creates a story, she (or he) has to figure out the structure she will use. She has to include certain sentences that will give the reader information about the theme, setting or plot. She might use a chapter to set the scene for what will follow in the rest of a book, include a pivotal scene that will develop the plot or theme, or use a stanza that is filled with images that would help the reader of a poem understand the theme of the work. Writers of stories or poems want to develop their plot, setting and theme, so they have to come up with a structure that allows them to do so. It is up to the reader to analyze the work and to respond to what the writer has written.

EXPLAIN HOW THE FOLLOWING EXCERPT WOULD CONTRIBUTE TO THE DEVELOPMENT OF THE SETTING AND PLOT.

> His mother tied the cap beneath his chin. Then she pulled the zipper up on his coat as far as it would go. She put his gloves on. They walked the distance to the pond. The ice was frozen solid. "It's time to learn how to stand on skates," she said to her son.

The excerpt clearly sets the stage for the story. It gives the reader clues about where and when the action is taking place. The mother is dressing her son warmly. They walk to a pond. It is frozen. It is clearly winter and the mother is going to show her son how to skate. This excerpt not only tells the reader where and when it takes place, it also contributes to the plot. It introduces two characters. The mother takes time to make sure her son is warm, implying that she is loving. Her son seems passive. Because she has to dress him, he must be little. So a relationship is also revealed in the excerpt that will doubtless influence the plot.

DISCUSS HOW THE FOLLOWING SENTENCE WOULD IMPACT THE THEME.

> Wanda realized then that she had made a terrible mistake and she would be haunted by the experience for the rest of her life.

This sentence would impact the theme because it suggests that Wanda would never recover from something that she did and that she would remember it for the rest of her life. This ties into a theme because it is saying something about life and what Wanda realizes about her life. We do not know what she did, but the sentence clearly states that it was a mistake. We would have to read the entire passage to understand why it was a mistake and why she would be haunted, but the sentence gives us a good idea that she learned a lesson from what happened.

Developing the Point of View of the Narrator or Speaker in a Text

An author uses many writing skills to develop a narrator's or speaker's point of view in a piece of literature. One way to develop a point of view is by having the narrator describe an event or a character. Or the author can choose to display a speaker's viewpoint through dialogue; a lot can be learned by what a character says. The manner in which the author reveals the narrator's or speaker's viewpoint may be subtle or it may be obvious. If it is done subtly, the reader will need to look for clues that help tell what the speaker's attitude is. That is why it is so important to study the language of the author, in order to analyze the narrator's or speaker's viewpoint about a character, event or topic.

Read the Following Excerpt and Analyze the Narrator's Viewpoint of Bonita.

> Bonita always wanted to make a difference. So it was no surprise when she spent hours after school as a volunteer at the hospital when she was in high school. Then, in college, she tutored children at a local center and later worked as a nurse in Africa. She was special.

The narrator seems to like Bonita. He says that Bonita "always wanted to make a difference," and that it was "no surprise" that she volunteered at the hospital. To make his point even greater, he says that she tutored children when she was in college and later worked as a nurse in Africa. The narrator ends the excerpt by calling Bonita "special," so it is clear that he likes her. He would not say that otherwise. When determining a narrator's viewpoint of a character, be sure to watch for clues that tell you the narrator's opinion, such as the clues in this excerpt.

Analyzing the Difference Between Reading, Hearing or Watching a Story, Drama, or Poem

When you read a story, drama, or poem rather than hear or watch it, certain elements will be lacking. While the act of reading is a rewarding one, it is very private and subjective. When the same story is made into a video, a whole new range of senses are encountered. The characters will be real people and their actions and reactions to events will be that much more exciting. And the story will seem that much more real. Certainly hearing a poem read can be more powerful than simply reading it. Poets' words are meant to be heard and the effect of that language is much more meaningful when it is read aloud by a powerful speaker. As for dramas, they are meant to be heard or seen. Reading them is enjoyable, but subtleties are often overlooked. When a reader actually hears the dialogue of a play, it will have a deeper meaning. Seeing a drama brought to life is far more enthralling than reading it.

Comparing and Contrasting a Story About Love and a Poem About Love

A story about love would involve characters and a plot. It would have events and probably a theme. It would look at love through the way the characters feel about it and what happens to them and what they say about it. In a poem, the speaker may be the only character. Rather than have a plot, a poem is much more likely to describe the effects of love in verse. Rather than having a conflict and events, a poem might be a tribute to love. Like a story, a poem would most likely have a theme. Some poems do have events and characters, but the emphasis is still on the language and, most of all, on figurative language. And a poem is much more likely to be read aloud than a story.

Historical Novel vs. Science Fiction Story

A historical novel is based on something that really happened; a science fiction story is not. A science fiction story is imaginary and probably contains components that are not based on reality. While a historical novel might deviate from the facts of a historical event by using fictional characters and dialogue, its basis is founded in historic fact. The science fiction genre only has fictional characters and situations that might be set in the past, but more likely in the future. It has nothing to do with the reality of a time or period, or if it does, it is only in passing.

Importance of Being Able to Read and Comprehend a Wide-Variety of Texts That Are at a Specific Grade Level

It is important that a student be able to read and comprehend literature including stories, dramas, and poems at a specific grade level to have success in school and later on in life. Being able to read a wide variety of texts will build vocabulary and create an appreciation for literature and other topics. Reading is proven to be a sure way to improve general education on many levels. It will allow the student to increase his or her ability to grab the essence of a book and to grow a vocabulary for words, both in understanding meaning and in spelling. It will also improve a student's grasp of grammar, language conventions, and good writing skills. Students can improve their reading gradually by keeping word lists and reading easier books until they are experienced enough to move to higher grade levels.

Informational Texts

Facts and Details

Explicit information is the facts and details that are stated in a passage. It is found directly in a text rather than being suggested or hinted at. Explicit information is frequently used to support a main idea and can be found just by reading through a text, especially an informational passage. *Inferences* are usually based on the explicit information in a passage. When making an inference, the reader needs to put together the pertinent explicit information to form a conclusion that was not explicit in the passage. It is the best guess that a reader can make based on the information given in a passage

Read the Following Excerpt. Tell Whether It Contains Explicit Information or Not.

> Oliver began to cut his way through the jungle. At first he was able to chop enough of the vines and bushes to make a narrow trail, but then the jungle became so thick that it was completely impassable. He had to return to camp and try to find another way to get to his destination.

Most of the information in the excerpt is explicit information. The information tells the reader about Oliver. It says that he was cutting his way through a jungle, but that the jungle became so thick that he couldn't get through and instead had to return to camp and find another way to get to where he wanted to go. All of the information is written right in the text. What is not clear is why Oliver was in the jungle and where he wanted to go. There is nothing in the explicit information to give us a hint about those questions.

Read the Passage and Discuss Why the Inference That the Disease Killed the Elm Trees Is Valid.

> Some years back, our towns were filled with elm trees. They grew tall and graceful. Some elm trees were hundreds of years old. Then a terrible disease came. Today elms are almost nonexistent in our towns.

When you make an inference, you need to look at the information in the passage. The passage said that years ago the towns were filled with elm trees. It tells the reader that the trees were graceful and some were hundreds of years old. It also says a terrible disease came and that today elms are almost gone. All of these details are explicit information. The reader can conclude from some of the information that the disease killed the elm trees. Using the facts that there were a lot of trees once, but not many today, you can infer that the disease killed them. This is not stated directly in the excerpt, but it is the best guess based on the information at hand.

Determining the Main Idea of a Passage

Main ideas are what a passage is mostly about. It is the central idea of a text, the overall idea that a reader comes away with after reading a passage, and why the passage is written. A main idea is not a detail. Details in a passage may support a main idea by telling more about it, but they are not the main idea itself. Passages may have more than one main idea and paragraphs may have a main idea of their own.

Identify and Explain the Main Idea of the Following Excerpt.

> People's permanent teeth should last forever. Unfortunately, many people don't clean them well. They don't brush or floss enough. They eat a lot of sweet foods. Because of this, their teeth decay. Their gums become diseased. Some people have very few teeth left when they turn 60.

The main idea is that people don't take care of their permanent teeth enough. The author tells us this is various ways. The excerpt says that people don't clean them well and that they don't brush or floss enough. It also says that teeth and gums decay because of the sweet foods people eat. These are the details that support the main idea. The main idea is found in the details. When analyzing which statement is a main idea, make sure to choose one that has a broad message, not one that is talking about something specific.

Objective Summary

An objective summary always includes the main idea and the most important details about the main idea. It does not include all of the supporting details. That would make the summary too long and more like a paraphrase of the text. A paraphrase includes a lot more information than a summary. When choosing which details to include, choose those that are most related to the main idea and are the most pertinent. Leave out those that are secondary. An objective summary does not include personal opinions; it is free of personal prejudice. It does not include judgments either.

Discovering Why the Summary Below Is Not Objective

> Many circus performers, like the lion tamer, the high wire performers, and the person who is shot out of a cannon, face dangers every day. But their love of the circus keeps them from leaving their jobs. That seems to be a silly choice to make in life.

This summary has a main idea and important details. The main idea is that circus performers face dangers every day. The details that are included are that the lion tamer, the high wire performers, and the person who is shot out of a cannon are among those performers who face the most danger. These are important details, so this part of the summary is excellent. But the summary is not objective because it also contains a judgment: "That seems to be a silly choice to make in life" has nothing to do with the main idea. It is the opinion of the reader and keeps the summary from being objective. Judgments and opinions that belong to the reader have no place in a summary.

Anecdotes and Examples as a Way of Introducing, Illustrating, or Elaborating Key Ideas in a Nonfiction Passage

Examples and anecdotes are two fine tools for introducing, illustrating, or elaborating key ideas in a passage. Anecdotes and examples provide the reader with a concrete means of understanding what the abstract idea means in terms of daily lives. Anecdotes in particular make complicated notions accessible so that they are easily grasped by the reader. For instance, telling a personal story about yourself not being able to understand instructions might help to illustrate why putting together a bicycle is difficult to do. Examples can consist of quotations from authorities as well as first-person interviews and primary sources. All of this helps to enlighten a reader about main ideas.

Read the passage and explain the meaning of "corresponds to."

> Computers can do a fine job of matching single people. They match people first on the basis of age so they will compatible. Most people want to date someone whose age corresponds to their own. Then computers pair off people by physical qualities like height, weight, hair and eyes.

To figure out the meaning of the phrase "corresponds to," the reader needs to look for context clues the same way the reader would try to figure out the meaning of a single word. The excerpt says that computers match people first on the basis of age so that they will be compatible. This is a context clue for the meaning of the term "corresponds to." Being compatible means getting along. Most people like to be with people around their same age, so this helps the reader decide that "corresponds to" means "resembles" in this usage. If the reader substitutes this word for the words "corresponds to," it makes sense.

Read the excerpt below and, using context clues, determine what the word "ostentatious" means.

> If movie stars wear too much expensive clothes and jewelry at one time, it makes them look ostentatious, which many people find unappealing because it makes the stars look cheap.

A good way to figure out the meanings of words and expressions without having to read their definitions in the dictionary is to use context clues. The way to discover context clues is to study the text. The excerpt says that if movie stars wear a lot of expensive clothes and jewelry at one time, many people think they look cheap. So the word "ostentatious" must link these two thoughts together. Wearing too much of anything that is expensive could be considered "showy." If you substitute the word "showy" for "ostentatious," it makes sense in the context of the sentence. This is the way you can work out the meaning of a word from context clues.

Figurative Language

Authors often make use of a technique that is called *figurative language*. Figurative language allows the writer to expand the way in which he or she uses language. Figurative language uses words in a non-literal way; this means that the word or expression takes on a new meaning. For instance, an author might say that Anthony is like Superman. While, everyone knows that Anthony isn't really like Superman because he does not have super powers, the image of Anthony as Superman changes the reader's impression of Anthony. Figurative language takes many forms; it can be in the form of a simile, a metaphor, and personification. *Similes* compare things using the comparing words "like" or "as," for example, "Anthony is like Superman." *Metaphors* compare things without using comparing words, for example, "Anthony is Superman when it comes to helping others." And *personification* gives a thing or animal human traits, for example, "The future called out to Anthony."

Discuss the kind of figurative language used in the following poem by the Scottish poet Robert Burns:

O my luve's like a red, red rose
That's newly sprung in June;
O my luve's like the melodie
That's sweetly played in tune.

The poet uses similes to create an image in this poem. There are two similes used here and they make up the entire poem: he says that his love is "like a red, red rose" and that she is also "like the melodie." These are examples of similes because they use the comparing word "like" to compare two things. They are not metaphors because metaphors do not use the comparing words "like" or "as." The poem paints an image of the poet's love by comparing her to a red rose that has newly sprung and a melodie that is sweetly played.

READ THE FOLLOWING PASSAGE AND DISCUSS HOW TO FIGURE OUT THE MEANING OF THE TECHNICAL TERM "SEISMOGRAPH."

> Karin knew this was a big earthquake, but she didn't realize how big until she started to check the readings on the seismograph. She was startled by what she read and quickly called Dr. Kai to alert him about her findings. They both studied the record carefully and then called the governor.

While a reader may not know the meaning of the technical term "seismograph," he could get a very good idea of its meaning from the context of the sentences around it. The first context clue is that Karin was checking the seismograph to find out how big an earthquake was, which must mean that a seismograph is some kind of scientific tool. She was startled by the findings of this machine, so it must have somehow managed to measure the extent of the earthquake. Through logic, a reader could figure out that a seismograph measures the intensity of earthquakes.

CONNOTATIONS OF "KEEN" VS. "PASSIONATE"

The word "passionate" suggests the state of being very involved in something, as in "liking something with a passion." The word "keen" is much less emphatic; someone who is keen about something likes it, but does not exhibit a passionate love of it. "Keen" suggests a mental state while "passionate" suggests an emotional state. Connotations carry many secondary meanings, so it is important to choose words that fit the situation. They are also filled with subtle overtones that should be analyzed and understood before choosing a word for use. Someone may be keen about a book or a dress, but it is doubtful that a person would be passionate about it.

STRUCTURE OF A TEXT

A good writer knows that every part of a text should fit together and have a purpose. For instance, writers often use a topic sentence at the start of a text to set the stage for the reader and alert her about what the topic is that the text will address. Writers use paragraphs to address different aspects of an overlying main idea. If the piece is long enough, chapters can be used to break up material so that it is more easily understood and found by a reader. There are other kinds of structuring a text too. A paper might be divided into sections for greater clarity. These techniques give writers greater flexibility and allow a writer to order a text in a logical and easier-to-read form.

VERONICA HAS BEEN DOING A LOT OF RESEARCH ON FROGS AND WANTS TO INCLUDE DATA ON SEVERAL DIFFERENT KINDS OF FROGS FOR A REPORT. WHAT KIND OF STRUCTURE MIGHT BE USEFUL FOR VERONICA TO USE?

The best choice for Veronica would probably be to divide her paper into sections, with each section having paragraphs that contain information about each type of frog. This would allow the reader to easily find information that he or she might be seeking and would act as a natural organizer for Veronica. She might include subheads with the name of each different kind of frog at the beginning of each section as well. She could also use subheads above a paragraph or a group of paragraphs, identifying the kind of information that is present there. And she could also include a topic sentence in each section or paragraph to tell what it is mostly about.

DETERMINING AN AUTHOR'S POINT OF VIEW

An author's point of view may be stated in a passage or it may be hidden or vaguely suggested. A student needs to read the text very closely to analyze what an author feels about her subject. When reading, look for any obviously emotional or opinionated statements. See what the author seems to have sympathy for. Some authors make their viewpoints very clear by stating it at the beginning or ending of a text, while others may want to keep their own opinions somewhat secret for many possible reasons. For example, many newspapers maintain a policy of unbiased reporting; even if a reporter has strong feelings, it may be nearly impossible to determine his point of view. Columnists, on the other hand, make their opinions very obvious. It is important to understand the author's viewpoint to ensure that you are reading something that gives a total picture of the topic without bias.

READ THE FOLLOWING EXCERPT FROM A MOVIE REVIEW AND DESCRIBE THE AUTHOR'S VIEWPOINT.

> The script, also by a newcomer, Alex Brandeis, is taut and suspenseful; however, the plot does seem to be a bit familiar. It's a story that seems to occur in the movies from time to time. Even so, this movie will leave you clutching your seat the whole time.

The author gives several hints about her viewpoint. First she says the script is taut and suspenseful, which suggests that she likes it. Then she says that the plot seems to be familiar, a sign that she is somewhat critical of the movie. She goes on to comment that the story has been repeated, but the final sentence makes it clear that the author's viewpoint about the movie is positive because she says "this movie will leave you clutching your seat the whole time." To determine an author's viewpoint, you need to examine and analyze the clues that an author gives you about what he or she is feeling.

DETERMINING THE PURPOSE OF A TEXT

When reading, the reader should always determine the purpose of a text. To do so, ask yourself what effect the writing has on you. Does the text try to explain or persuade you of something? Perhaps the text is making an appeal to your emotions. The signs that a text is attempting to persuade you include an author offering an opinion and explaining why she thinks this way. On the other hand, if a text is simply informative, it will have many facts that will give details about an event or person or a thing, but not try to persuade you of anything. Manuals that come with equipment are clearly not persuasive, simply instructive.

EXPLAIN THE PURPOSE OF THE PASSAGE BELOW.

> Remember, no matter who you support, you have a duty as an American to voice your opinion on Tuesday. This is a privilege that so many people in other countries do not have, so make sure you get to your local polling place.

The purpose of the excerpt is to convince people to vote. This is clearly what the author wants to happen. He gives an argument for voting when he says it is your "duty as an American." He reasserts his purpose by telling people to "get to your local polling place." He uses reasons that he feels are important to urge people to vote, noting that many people in other countries do not have the same "privilege" of being able to vote for the candidate they choose. The author does not urge a particular person or party to vote for, simply that you should vote. This piece is meant to persuade.

INTEGRATING INFORMATION PRESENTED IN DIFFERENT MEDIA OR FORMATS WITH WORDS TO DEVELOP A COHERENT UNDERSTANDING OF A TOPIC

When researching a topic or issue, you may find various ways that information is presented. It may be in written form, in a text; it may be in a visual form, including charts, lists or even videos. The way in which to come to an understanding of the information is to combine it as best as possible. While a text may have the larger picture about an issue, a chart could give you more specific information about one aspect of the issue at hand. A cartoon, for example, could give you a perspective that an informational report would not. Lists may help you categorize information about a topic and videos may give you a different perspective of the importance of an issue. Each representation has its place and it is important to use the benefit of the variety of presentations that exist to enhance your understanding of a topic.

ANALYZING AN ARGUMENT

When reading a persuasive text, the first thing a reader should do is follow the way in which the author is building the argument. Look for the main contention that the author has and also the ways in which the author adds to her argument. Usually the author will include supporting information to her claims, but that supporting information needs to be valid in order to support the claim. Look at the supporting evidence and notice where it comes from. Ask yourself if the evidence is based on facts and if the facts come from a reliable source or from a source that cannot be researched and confirmed. Be cautious of emotional claims that are based more on feelings than on fact. Throw out any claims that lack proper verification.

READ THE EXCERPT AND ANALYZE THE AUTHOR'S CLAIM.

> We at Woodcrest Middle School should be more aware of our environment. We need to practice more recycling. It is important to our environment. According to an article written by ecologist Dr. Sam Schwartz, if every one of us recycled our school paper, we would see a 20 percent reduction in the waste at our school. So let's start today.

The author is claiming that recycling is important to the environment. He wants school students to recycle more. He uses supporting information from an article by ecologist Dr. Sam Schwartz. The fact that he has a doctorate degree is a good sign, but it would be better to find out where the article was published and a few more of his credentials as an expert. The author of the excerpt might have added these details to strengthen his claim. On the surface, however, the claim seems valid. The author does not use emotional appeals. The piece is quite straightforward and that is a good sign in such a text.

MEMOIR VS. BIOGRAPHY

A memoir written by a person would include many intimate details about the person's feelings that a biographer might only guess at. The format would be much more personal than the format of a biography as well. The word *memoir* is French for "memory" and that is what a memoir is—the memories of an individual about his or her life. A biography would, by its very nature, be more formal than a memoir. A biographer is limited by the information he can research—and if the biographer is lucky enough to be able to interview the subject himself, the writer could add more personal details. Still, the biography would be written in the third person, which would give it more distance from the subject than a memoir would. On the other hand, a memoir can be very similar to an autobiography, which is written by the subject herself.

IMPORTANTANE OF BEING A PROFICIENT READER OF NONFICTION TEXTS

Being a proficient reader is essential to success at school and later in life, both in grade 6 and beyond. Comprehension of a wide range of nonfiction texts gives a student the ability to be at ease in reading schoolbooks and other texts throughout his life. Whether reading a science book, a newspaper, a railroad schedule or an instruction manual, a good reader will be able to interpret and find the information that is needed. Becoming a good reader involves reading a lot, looking up the meaning of words, and keeping word lists. This scaffolding will help improve the reading of any student and make him prepared for more difficult academic challenges.

Writing

PRODUCING CLEAR AND COHERENT WRITING

The first step to producing clear and coherent writing is to plan what you want to write about, what your purpose will be, and who your audience will be. Do you want to explain an idea? Do you want to persuade your audience? Do you want to entertain? These are all considerations when deciding on a purpose. Once you have settled on a purpose, you will need to develop the presentation by figuring out how to organize it and deciding on a style. A style should be chosen that fits with the purpose of the text and its audience. If you are writing a formal report, you need to adopt a formal style of writing. However, if you are writing something more casual, and your audience expects a casual approach, then there is no need for a formal style. Whatever the purpose or audience, your text should include proper English grammar and have a beginning, middle, and ending.

CONSTRUCTIVE CRITICISM

Writing is an ongoing process in that it needs to be revised, edited and possibly rewritten before it is completed. This process can be a difficult one, so it is wise to have the support of peers and adults who can objectively critique your work. The first thing to do when writing a text is to know what you want to say and then write a rough draft. Sit with it for a few hours or days, and then revisit it and make any changes that you think will improve it. Then ask a friend or an adult, a teacher perhaps, to read the text and critique it. Their feedback will be very useful, and you will probably want to revise or rewrite based on what they say. At some point, the text may need to be edited for improper language. Make sure that your use of pronouns is precise and correct and that you double check your spelling before you are finished.

USING THE INTERNET

The technology of the Internet has changed the way in which writing can be produced and published. Self-publishing sites abound on the Internet and many people produce e-books with ease. But that is just one aspect. For students, technology allows for easy access to sources used in a writing project. These sources can be cited by listing the URL, title, author, and date retrieved. Once written, you can post your writing on a blog and then you can discuss it in one of the many chat rooms and topic websites. These tools allow for an unprecedented exchange of information. In addition, many free tools are accessible that provide software to allow people to work together on a wide variety of projects, no matter how far apart they are geographically. Students can find discussion groups, file sharing networks, social networking sites, blogs and task management sites, all of which foster interaction and collaboration.

CONDUCTING A SHORT RESEARCH PROJECT

To conduct a short research project to answer a question, it is best to begin by creating a list of key words that can be entered into an Internet search engine to find the information you are seeking from an online source, such as an encyclopedia, journals, magazines, and other available sources. You may have to refine and refocus your inquiry if you do not find the exact information you want—sometimes a simple rewriting of the keyword will bring up more information than what appeared in the first search. Whatever information you plan to use to answer the question should be cited correctly following the standards of the MLA (Modern Language Association).

Your teacher wants you to find the answer to the question, "Who discovered America?" Discuss how to go about finding the answer.

The best way to learn who discovered America is to start with an Internet search. You would need to come up with keywords for a search engine. You could simply type in the question for a start and that would lead to an enormous amount of information. You could change the keywords by searching for "America discoverer," or "American discovery" to see if this yields other information. Check out the websites and make sure they are reliable and accredited. Pick sites that are related to historic groups or affiliated with colleges or universities or other credible sources. And be sure to credit your sources when you write your answer.

Gathering Relevant Information from Multiple Print and Digital Sources

After doing research through an online search for information on a topic and a visit to the school library for research on the same subject in the print resources there, you will need to make a list of your sources with the information you gathered from each and review the sources to see whether they are credible. Credible sources will have legitimacy to them; they could be related to a university, a historic society, or a scientific group. Delete any sources that are suspect. Then, when you start to write your essay, make sure you do not copy any of the information from a site or print source verbatim; that is, you need to paraphrase the information so that it is not plagiarized. By putting your own spin on the material, avoiding such plagiarism can usually be accomplished fairly easily. You may wish to include quotations from experts, in which case you must cite the quote. At the end of your paper, you should include all sources and properly cite them using the MLA (Modern Language Association) standards.

Importance of Varying Sentence Patterns When Writing

Readers become bored with what they are reading if the way in which it is written is dull and repetitive. One short sentence after another will not appeal to the average reader, nor would one long sentence after another. Written text should have variety. Sentences should be both simple and complex and the syntax should change as you write. This gives the writing life and rhythm. You can interject variety by combining multiple short sentences into one long sentence through the use of clauses and phrases. Mix in a handful of direct short sentences to break up a pattern of too many long sentences. A good tip is to read what you have written aloud and see if it has a pleasing rhythm.

Discuss how to rewrite the sentences below to make them more varied.

> Andre and Susan went to Cape Cod last week. They hoped to see a cranberry harvest. But they arrived too early in the season. The harvest would not take place for another month. They were disappointed when they left.

All of the sentences in the excerpt are about the same length and follow the same pattern. They are monotonous because of a lack of variety. The use of clauses and phrases to combine information would improve the flow of the words. One way that they could be rewritten to make them more interesting is the following:

> Andre and Susan went to Cape Cod last week hoping to see a cranberry harvest. They were disappointed, however, because the harvest would not take place for another month. They arrived too early in the season.

This version has rhythm and variety in the sentences. A reader would be more interested in reading the entire excerpt because of this.

Importance of Maintaining a Consistent Style and Tone

When writing, it is important to maintain a consistent style and tone. For instance, if you are writing a formal report, you should maintain a formal style and tone of writing. To suddenly have a section of the paper that uses informal language and a casual tone would not fit into the completed text. In the same manner, if you are writing a story about a ten-year-old girl, the language that you have her use should be consistent with words that she would understand. The style and tone of a story tell you a lot about the narrator, so it is important to be consistent in order for the reader to understand what you are attempting to say.

Ways the Approach Used in a Poem on a Subject Might Be Different from the Approach Used to Write a Story About the Same Subject

Poetry is very different from stories; poems do not usually tell a story or have many characters, although some do. Poems are more concerned about creating a mood, drawing a picture, and giving a reader images that will have an emotional effect. Stories can also set moods and have an emotional effect, but the intent of a story is to describe something that happened. Most stories have plots and characters who reveal themselves and interact with the events in the story. Both poems and stories can have themes. For instance, a poem about a walk in the woods might not have much action, but it would probably create a sensation of what it feels like to be walking in the woods. A story about walking in the woods would most likely address not only the setting, but also the events that occur during the walk and how the characters react to them.

Using Critical Reading Skills

When reading nonfiction pieces, you should analyze the author's point of view. Then you need to assess the author's claims and see if the evidence given is sound and relevant. In a way, you will need to be a detective. This requires using critical reading skills. You need to figure out if the reasoning is sound. Ask yourself if what the author says is based on fact or unjustified opinion. Distinguish between statements by determining if they are based on fact or opinion. Check the sources that are cited. Look for evidence of bias, omissions and stereotypes; their presence severely distorts a work of nonfiction.

Making Writing a Habit

Writing is important both in school and in life. It is essential to learn to write routinely so that writing comes easily and smoothly. You can make writing a habit by doing it every day in some way. Certainly it is true that the more you write the better your writing will become. Familiarize yourself with the process of writing—taking notes, writing drafts, rewriting, editing, and revising once again—and you will come to understand the concept of writing for different kinds of audiences. Some writing needs to be longer and more thoroughly researched. Other writing can be shorter. It depends on the topic, the audience, and how complex you wish to be. Learning the skills necessary to master the art of writing for specific reasons will lead to greater recognition in any field you choose.

Persuasive Text

Introducing Claims and Organizing Reasons and Evidence That Support the Claims Clearly

When introducing claims in a persuasive text, be sure that the claim is thoroughly researched and thought through. You should have clear evidence that your claim is valid. The best way to do this is to make notes or an outline. When writing, organize your passage so that your claim comes first and then list the reasons and evidence that you have to support the claim. Make sure the reasons and evidence follow from each other so that they are in a clear order. Delete any claims that you cannot verify by reliable outside sources. By doing this you will be able to write a convincing presentation based on sound research.

ANALYZE THE CLAIM MADE IN THE STATEMENT BELOW.

The idea of building a minor league baseball stadium is a good one. It could be used not only by a farm team, but also for concerts. It is sure to attract people and help the town's economy. So vote yes at the polls on the referendum.

This claim may or may not be valid. While the statement says that the baseball stadium will attract people and be good for the town's economy, it does not provide any concrete evidence for the claim. There is no way to know whether building a baseball stadium would attract people. There are no facts or figures from other places that have already built a similar stadium, so the evidence is not based on anything credible. When making a claim, the argument should be well researched and sources used to back up the claim and make it a valid one. This is not the case in the statement that was given.

When making a claim you will need to research arguments in support of it that come from trustworthy sources. It is not enough to research a claim on the Internet because many Internet sources are dubious. If you are doing research on the Internet, then you will need to find information that can be verified by several objective sites. Another avenue is to find authorities in a field that have written or spoken on the topic that you are presenting so that you can quote these people. These authorities should have substantial degrees in their field as well as a vast experience so that their opinions will have credence and respect. Be sure to cite any information that you use to support a claim correctly. And make sure to present your arguments in a logical manner so that they will be easily understood by the listener or reader.

USE WORDS, PHRASES AND CLAUSES TO CLARIFY THE RELATIONSHIP BETWEEN CLAIMS AND REASONS

When writing, it is important to phrase your sentences so that the relationship between claims and reasons is clear. Words or phrases such as "because," "since, "as a result of," and "as a consequence" or "consequently" all suggest a causality that may exist between a claim and a reason. Clauses can also be utilized to show relationships. For example, the sentence "We are going to lose the election as a result of not working hard enough to convince the public" shows causality between the claim and the reason. When writing, make sure to recheck your sentences to ensure that there is a natural flow and that the relationships between claims and reasons are clear and logical.

CHOOSE WHICH OF THE FOLLOWING WORDS FITS BEST IN THE BLANK AND WHY: "OTHERWISE" OR "BECAUSE."

The jury found the defendant not guilty ______ the testimony of the eyewitness was weak.

"Because" is the correct choice because it shows a cause and effect relationship. "Otherwise" shows a relationship of contrast which is not the case here. It is important to understand the relationship between what happened as a result of something else. Using the correct linking word clarifies meaning and gives your sentences a logical flow. "Otherwise" suggests a relationship that exists between opposing possibilities. But this is not the case here. Using the word "because" gives the sentence a natural and logical flow.

FORMAL STYLE

When writing any kind of formal paper, a *formal style* of writing needs to be established and maintained throughout. A formal writing style includes the use of the third person, rather than first or second person. This lends a more serious and objective tone to a paper; personal feelings have little place in formal writing. A formal style also requires proper English conventions as well as language that is professional and specific. Generally idioms and contractions have no place when using a formal writing style, which requires that the author be objective and professional.

READ THE FOLLOWING LINES. SUGGEST HOW TO MAKE THEM MORE FORMAL.

> Turtles are something I like. They're reptiles and breathe. They have lungs like me. Some turtles breathe underwater. I've read that turtles eat many things like insects and fish and fruit too! Some turtles sleep underwater too.

The style of the passage is very informal and personalized; the first person is used exclusively. Sentences are all short and simple, and there is little substance.

HERE IS ONE WAY TO REWRITE IT:

> Turtles are interesting animals. They are reptiles and they breathe. They have lungs like humans do. Some turtles breathe underwater. They may sleep underwater too. They eat many things, including insects, fish, and fruit.

To give the passage a more formal tone, the first person is replaced by the third person. The organization is better because related information is put together, such as the fact that some turtles can both breathe and sleep underwater. The contraction was eliminated, as well as the reference to having lungs "like me." The exclamation mark also does not have a place in formal writing because it suggests feelings rather than logic.

GOOD CONCLUDING STATEMENT

It is important that a writer include a good concluding statement or section that follows from an argument in order to sum up a claim and review the intention of the text. This will give the audience a sense of closure. The conclusion or section should go over the most important points that were made in the persuasive text as well as the reasons and arguments made by the author in a brief form. The conclusion should make the reader feel that he or she has a firm understanding of the issue. A good conclusion is important to the effectiveness of a text.

VERONICA IS WRITING A PERSUASIVE PASSAGE ON WHY SHE BELIEVES THAT STUDENTS SHOULD GO TO SCHOOL ALL YEAR LONG. SHE NEEDS A CONCLUDING STATEMENT. DESCRIBE HOW SHE SHOULD GO ABOUT WRITING A CONCLUSION.

Veronica should review the arguments that she has made about what the benefits of going to school all year long are and the sources that she used to prove her point. She should also make a general statement about why she feels it would be a good idea. A personal appeal and an explanation of the benefits this approach would have could be used. It is probably best not to include too much about opposing points of view in the conclusion. The conclusion that Veronica writes should give the reader a sense of closure and satisfaction. It should not introduce new material or leave items open for further discussion.

Informational or Explanatory Text

INTRODUCING A TOPIC

When writing an informational or explanatory text, the author will need to introduce the topic that the text will be about. There are numerous strategies that can help improve the reader's comprehension of the subject. An author may choose to define key words that a reader may not be familiar with, classify information or compare and contrast it, or use a cause and effect relationship in the report. Charts and tables are extremely useful for displaying complicated information and the use of headings can help signify where certain information will be found. Multimedia devices, including video and audio, can also improve the way in which an author displays his material because they are appealing to the audience or reader.

SARA IS WRITING A REPORT ON SEA TURTLES. SHE HAS RESEARCHED THE VARIOUS DANGERS THAT THEY FACE: THEIR PREDATORS, THE DIFFICULTIES THEY ENCOUNTER IN THEIR LIFE CYCLE STARTING WITH THEIR BIRTH, THEIR MIGRATION TO THE OCEAN, AND THE DANGERS THAT AWAIT THEM AS THEY MATURE. SHE IS UNSURE OF HOW TO ORGANIZE HER REPORT.

Explain which organization pattern would be the best choice for her and why.

A cause and effect order would seem to be the best idea for Sara because she would be able to identify the causes and effects of the dangers that sea turtles encounter. She could organize the report so that each paragraph deals with a different threat, using headings to identify what would be in each section. A chart would also be useful because it puts the same information in a clear format so that readers would be able to refer to it. She might also consider using a video showing baby turtles migrating towards the open sea, which would give her audience an even greater understanding of the turtles' plight.

DEVELOPING A TOPIC

To develop a topic in an informational or explanatory text, an author needs to use relevant facts that support details related to the main topic. The topic may be included in a topic sentence or opening statement and then followed by supporting details. Some of the supporting details should be concrete facts that have been researched and confirmed. Quotations of experts in the field of the topic are another good source for supporting material. Quoting experts gives variety and credence to a text. Examples, charts, and multimedia techniques can also be used to enhance the presentation, but these extras should not be used as a substitute for solid supporting details.

ANALYZE THE BEGINNING OF THIS INFORMATIONAL TEXT AND TELL WHAT COULD BE ADDED TO IMPROVE IT.

> The journey of the salmon from salt water to fresh water to breed is one of the wonders of nature. This journey, called the salmon run, is difficult because the fish must swim upriver against the current. Some even leap up waterfalls as they make their way back to their original breeding grounds.

This seems like a good start to an informational text. The first sentence establishes the topic. It tells what the report is going to be about. It also includes two supporting details to tell more about the topic. This is one way to introduce and develop a topic in a report or other informational or explanatory text. What should come next are more supporting details and also sources for the information that is cited; a quotation from an authority of the salmon run would make the report stronger and give it credence. Some statistics, facts, figures about how many salmon make the run each year and how many survive would also be of interest.

USING APPROPRIATE TRANSITIONS

When writing an informational or explanatory text it is important to use appropriate transitions that will clarify the relationships among ideas and concepts. For example, to show causality between ideas, use transition words or phrases, such as "therefore," "consequently," and "as a result of." To show comparison or contrast relationships, words such as "however," "on the other hand," "but," "in contrast," and "similarly" should be used. Transition words and expressions to introduce examples include "for example, "for instance," "namely" and "that is." The order of importance can also be shown through transitions, such as "at first," "former," "latter," "primarily" and "second."

Importance of Using Precise Language and Domain-Specific Vocabulary

When writing informational or explanatory texts it is of utmost importance to use precise language and domain-specific vocabulary to explain your main idea and supporting details. Generalized vocabulary will not help the audience grasp the points that you are attempting to make because they will not accurately reflect your main idea and supporting details. Domain-specific vocabulary is important to use because it will accurately describe or explain the ideas or processes that are central to your text. When you research a subject, make sure to familiarize yourself with any vocabulary that is involved in its explanation. Use context clues, dictionaries, or, if necessary, a technical dictionary to decode any words that you are not familiar with. Also include definitions of domain-specific vocabulary in your text to enlighten readers.

Establishing and Maintaining a Formal Style

When writing an informational or explanatory text it is important to establish and maintain a formal style of writing. Do not use a colloquial or casual tone. It is necessary to use the third person and to make the sentences longer and more complex. It is also important not to use contractions when you write. A formal style announces that the writer is serious about his or her subject and wants to write an objective paper. This can be done by keeping the main ideas and supporting details clear, to the point, but as complex as they need to be. A formal style also means that the writer will not include a personal opinion that is not justified.

Discuss why the following excerpt is an example of formal writing.

> Richard Spruce found his life's work in the jungles of South America. Spruce grew up in a part of England that was filled with plants growing wild and free. His love of plants developed early. When he read a book about the Amazon jungle in Brazil, he decided to go there to study the area's plant life.

This is a good example of formal writing. It is objective and unbiased. The author uses the third person perspective, which formal writing is supposed to do. He sets out his main idea in the initial topic sentence, and then gives good supporting details. His sentences are somewhat complex and varied. He does not use any contractions, which are not used in formal writing, and the language is not colloquial or casual. The style of writing matches the subject. At the same time, the writing is not dull; the reader is intrigued and wants to learn more. Formal writing does not have to be uninteresting.

Importance of a Concluding Statement

A concluding statement or section that follows from and supports the information or explanation is important to a text because the conclusion helps to focus the important points in a text and also provides closure to the reader or audience. A good conclusion attempts to sum up the passage and any conclusions that the author makes so that the audience feels they have received a logical ending to the text. An effective conclusion gives the passage the weight it needs to have an effect. The conclusion should not make the reader feel that there is more information to follow, but rather set the tone for the ending of the topic.

Narratives

Establishing a Context and Introducing a Narrator and/or Characters

When writing a narrative, an author must establish the context of the story, which means he needs to set the stage for the story to begin. Sometimes this is done by establishing the setting of the story and then introducing a narrator and characters. Sometimes a character or the narrator is introduced first. A narrator and/or characters can be introduced in many ways: through the use of dialogue, through description, or through the reactions of the narrator or characters to an event. Whatever means an author chooses needs to call out to the audience so that they will be immediately interested in what is happening in the narrative. The beginning of a narrative must be compelling so that a reader will continue.

Discuss the introduction of the character in the following passage.

> Her parents named her Milagro, which means "miracle" in Spanish, but they called her Milly. She was a premature baby, very tiny, and it was a miracle that she survived. That was the beginning of her good fortune.

The author uses a dramatic way to introduce her character. She tells us that "Milagro" means "miracle" in Spanish. She tells us that it was a miracle that she survived her birth because she was born prematurely. She tells us that that was the beginning of her good fortune, a piece of information that tempts the reader to keep reading and find out more about Milagro's life. The way Milagro is introduced is dramatic because the author uses information to hint at what may come next. This is a form of foreshadowing. The author has established an interesting beginning with the way in which she introduces this character.

Sequence of Events

A sequence of events in a narrative should come naturally and logically out of the action and the plot. The sequence should follow the natural flow of a dialogue or plot and enhance what happens in the story. This is generally the rule, although authors sometimes use a literary device called *flashback*, in which the sequence of events is presented out of order. A flashback shows the action that will take place in the future before the events that build up to it. But following a flashback, the order of events will return to normal. The order of events in a narrative is important in helping the reader understand the intent or message of a narrative. When reading a narrative, take note of the order in which events occur to give a broader understanding of the passage.

Techniques Used by an Author

Authors can choose from many techniques to bring their stories to life. Dialogue is an important tool; it not only tells you what is happening in a narrative, but it also suggests what a character's personality is like. The reader can tell from what a character says and how the character says it what the character feels about the events in a narrative or even what he feels about himself. Pacing is equally important; the pacing is the rhythm of a story. It can move slowly in one section and then speed up to build intensity. Descriptions that are vivid help the reader visualize what is happening and what a character is like. All of these techniques help color the experiences and events in a narrative and increase the receptivity of the reader.

Discuss the pacing in the following excerpt.

> The day was lazy and long and no one wanted to move around very much, even though they were supposedly hunting. And then, out of nowhere, a deer darted over the horizon. Joe and Neal jumped up. They were alert now. It was time to get going.

The pacing changes from a leisurely pace at the beginning to a quick pace. It parallels what is happening in the excerpt. At first there is nothing happening so the pace is slow and relaxed. But after the deer appears, the pace picks up and so does the action. The pace mirrors the plot. The pace is shown by the use of sentences. Long sentences give a slow feeling, while shorter sentences create a quicker pace and help build tension in the writing. A story's pacing creates its rhythm, and a reader should realize how that is affecting him.

Importance of Transition Words

Transition words are very important when writing a narrative. They can indicate a sequence of events and also signal shifts from one time frame or setting to another. Sequence words such as "first," "second," and "last" assist the reader in understanding the order in which events occur, which can be important to the flow of the plot. Words such as "then" or "next" also show the order in which events occur. "After a while" and "before this" are other sequence expressions. A change in setting can also be indicated. For instance, a passage may say, "At first we were sitting comfortably in the hotel lobby," but later on it might say, "after we talked, we went to the theater to watch the musical." This shows a shift in setting. When reading, notice transition words and their effect on the action.

Precise Language

It is important to use precise language and descriptions that are lively and thought provoking so that a reader can gain insight into a character or situation. Details of the setting, what characters do, or the events in a narrative should be described in vivid and sensory language. The more moving the writing, the more moved the reader will be. Sensory language in particular helps convey the mood and feeling of the setting, situation, and characters. All of this will add to the development of a memorable theme. When reading, take care to notice the selection of words and phrases that an author employs in order to better comprehend the meaning of a narrative.

Read the Excerpt and Analyze the Language.

> At dawn, in a stuffy and smoky second-class car in which five people had already spent the night, a bulky woman in deep mourning was hoisted in—almost like a shapeless bundle. Behind her, puffing and moaning, followed her husband—a tiny man, thin and weakly, his face death-white, his eyes small and bright and looking shy and uneasy.

The language selected by the author is filled with fresh and precise words that describe and color the two passengers as well as the setting of the excerpt. The author describes the car as "stuffy and smoky," "second-class," and "in which five people had already spent the night." All this conjures up a dreary train car. The author describes the woman as "a shapeless bundle." Her husband is "tiny," "thin," and "weakly" with a "death-white" face. These words not only lend freshness to the writing, they also clearly depict what the people look like for the reader. This is the way that a writer can color his story and the characters in it.

Role of a Conclusion

The conclusion to a narrative is extremely important. It is the resolution of the story and helps the reader decide on the theme or point of the narration. The conclusion to a narrative is the resolution of the problem that is faced by the characters. A conclusion may not always be apparent; it may leave some questions unanswered. Nevertheless, a conclusion should give the reader the sense that the narrative is over, whatever the outcome. And the outcome can vary: in tragedies the conclusion is always sad, while comedies always end with a light-hearted fashion. Unlike conclusions in traditional literature, conclusions in modern literature can be much more evasive, which often leaves the reader with more questions than answers. But even this helps form the narrative and give it meaning.

KEEGAN IS WRITING A STORY ABOUT A BOY WHO PUSHES HIMSELF TO BECOME AN ATHLETE. KEEGAN HAS WRITTEN ABOUT HOW HARD THE BOY HAS TRAINED FOR AN UPCOMING RACE. HE HAS NOTED THAT WINNING HAS BECOME A HUGE FORCE IN HIS LIFE. NOW KEEGAN IS TRYING TO COME UP WITH A CONCLUSION TO HIS STORY. DESCRIBE WHAT HE SHOULD LOOK FOR WHEN HE WRITES THE CONCLUSION.

Keegan should think about what the theme of the story is meant to be. Is it a story about someone who works hard and gets what he wants? Or is it about someone who loses an important race and how he deals with it? The theme should dictate the ending of the story in this case, whether he won or lost the race. A conclusion should bring the entire story to a fitting and appropriate ending so that the reader has a sense of closure. It should follow the opening and the many events that happen, so that there is a form to the story. And it should support the theme the author wants to teach.

Speaking and Listening

Discussions

Preparing for a Discussion on a Particular Topic

Class discussions are important tools because they allow peers to talk about a subject that they have researched and then exchange ideas about that subject. But the ideas that are exchanged should be related to concrete evidence that each student has discovered as a result of research. When preparing for a class discussion, it is necessary to thoroughly research the subject. Make sure you have read as much credible information that you can find. Make notes on the material, writing down pertinent information such as quotes, statistics, and other supporting evidence. It can be helpful to rehearse what you are planning to say by practicing with a family member or friend. Determine what you are going to focus on.

Engaging in Collegial Discussions

When engaging in collegial discussions, it is important to set specific goals and deadlines so that there will be a definite order to assist in making these forums productive. Rules for participants should be set beforehand as well as the goals and the amount of time that will be given to complete each goal. Progress towards reaching these goals should be tracked. Roles for everyone also need to be defined. Participants should learn how to use questions to add detail and depth to the discussion, and how to build on and further ideas that are put forth by others. It is important to learn to communicate with others who may have a different perspective. Everyone should be able to make use of evidence and to express themselves clearly.

Posing and Responding to Specific Questions with Elaboration and Detail

Asking questions in a discussion is an important technique that can be learned. The best kind of question to pose is one that requires the person who is answering to think about what was said and the evidence that he or she has that is relevant to the answer. Questions should focus on "how, what and why" and should be open-ended, which means they cannot be answered with one word. Questions should be based on the information that is being discussed and should be an extension of that material. Answering questions is equally artful because the person answering must consider all aspects of the issue and have on-hand evidence and information that will support the answer. Good questions and good answers do not stray off topic.

Reviewing Key Ideas and Viewpoints

A discussion should begin with the presentation of key ideas and the viewpoints of all participants. This will give every student a chance to reflect on what was said. At some predetermined point in the discussion, a review of all of the key ideas that have been stated should be reviewed. This will require proof that each student is able to paraphrase what other students have said. The review should be done in an orderly manner, with the student who originally put forth the idea reviewing the understanding of other students about what was said. This review can add clarity to the process of understanding others with different perspectives.

Interpreting Information

Interpreting information presented in diverse media and formats is an important skill to develop because the additional information can greatly enhance existing information on a particular topic. Students should become familiar with various media forms including interactive graphics, video, audio, and online sites so that they can make use of the information that is found within them. Once mastered, these things can be included in a presentation. Such a variety of formats is sure to enliven any presentation when speaking. But be sure that you understand the information, and how to use the technology, before you include it as an addition to your presentation.

Analyzing a Speaker's Argument and Claims

A speaker's argument and claims need to be evaluated for their soundness and relevance. While it is tempting to believe everything that an excellent speaker tells you, it is because of that excellence that a listener should be critical of everything that is being said. While listening, critique what the person is saying. Determine if there is a clear delineation between evidence and theory. If a statement is theoretical, is it identified as such or is it merely a rhetorical statement meant to sway you to the speaker's opinion? It is important that the argument provides sufficient evidence to convince you, the audience, of the validity of the claims being made. Make sure to determine whether the speaker's arguments are logical or emotional, and make sure there is sufficient reasoning to support any claims.

Presenting Claims and Findings, Sequence Ideas Logically, and Using Pertinent Descriptions

In a focused discussion, the attention should be paid to how claims and findings are presented and sequenced. Claims and findings should be supported by pertinent descriptions, facts, and details that support the main ideas and the themes. These supporting facts and details should follow in a logical manner so that the audience will be able to follow the argument. A speaker needs to organize his thoughts; making an outline is one helpful way to ensure that you will stay on subject. Details, descriptions, or facts that support the main claims should flow one from the other in a logical sequence. This will help the audience understand more completely what the speaker is saying.

Importance of Appropriate Eye Contact, Adequate Voice Volume, and Clear Pronunciation

There are many important skills that a speaker should master in order to be effective. Among these skills is learning how to make and maintain eye contact with the audience or with other participants. Maintaining eye contact assures a presentation that is believable and, more than likely, a presentation that will be remembered. Eye contact also makes the presentation personal, as though the speaker is speaking directly to someone. Also key to making a presentation successful is speaking in a clear voice; a voice should be loud and clear enough to be heard, but not so loud as to be unnecessarily distracting. The speaker should use clear diction and pronunciation as well to ensure that the audience understands what they are hearing. These skills are the hallmark of an effective presentation.

Using Multimedia Components and Visual Displays

Multimedia components and visual displays not only enhance presentations, they can make information much more understandable. For instance, if you are making a presentation about a complex subject, a visual display can show the way in which the material should come together. Multimedia components including graphics, diagrams, and charts also serve to reinforce spoken information. Certainly, many people learn more quickly when a visual presentation accompanies a verbal one. They also serve to break a presentation up so that it is more interesting to the viewer. However, these multimedia components are only aids; they cannot stand on their own. The speaker must bring them everything together with his verbal presentation.

ADAPTING SPEECH TO A VARIETY OF CONTEXTS AND TASKS TO DEMONSTRATE A COMMAND OF FORMAL ENGLISH

Learning to be poised when speaking in front of people is a daunting task, but one that can be learned through practice. Part of being able to stand before people and speak is learning confidence, and one way to learn confidence is to be able to demonstrate a good command of formal English. Certainly, the words you use in a presentation should vary according to the audience. You would not speak the same way to your peers as you might to an audience at a graduation ceremony, but in either case you will need to write out your presentation and revise it for any incorrect usages. Of particular concern is making sure that pronouns agree with one another. They must also be clearly linked to their antecedents so that the audience will be able to follow you. Once you have improved your presentation's English usage, try rehearsing it in front of a mirror. This will help you develop further confidence and poise.

Language

Pronouns

Pronouns can be subjective, objective or possessive. A *subjective pronoun* is a pronoun that takes the place of the noun that is the subject of a sentence. For example, in the sentence "They went for a trip to the country," the pronoun "they" is in the subjective pronoun. Other subjective pronouns are "I," "it," "you," "he," "she," and "we." An *objective pronoun* takes the place of the noun that is the predicate of a sentence. For example, in the sentence "Tom threw the baseball to him," the objective pronoun is "him." Other objective pronouns are "me," "it," "you," "her," "us," and "them." *Possessive pronouns* take the place of possessive nouns. In the sentence "Their coats were warm," The possessive pronoun is "their." Other possessive pronouns are "my," "mine," "his," "hers," "ours," and "yours."

Identify the errors in the following sentence and correct them.

Me and Billy are going to the football game with him brother.

There are two errors in pronoun usage in the sentence. The first one is the incorrect choice of an objective pronoun as a subject of the sentence. The "me" should be "I." This is the proper choice of pronoun for first person singular. Also, the placement of the pronoun is incorrect. It should follow the other part of the compound subject and read "Billy and I." The "him" before the word "brother" is also incorrect. This should be a possessive pronoun, but "him" is an objective pronoun. It is supposed to be the possessive pronoun "his." The revised sentence should read: "Billy and I are going to the football game with his brother."

Intensive pronouns are used to emphasize another pronoun or noun. They are formed by putting "self" after objective pronouns, such as "myself," "yourself," "herself," "himself," "itself," "ourselves," "yourselves" and "themselves." For example, the following sentence uses an intensive pronoun for emphasis: "Desiree is going to lead the parade herself." When these pronouns are used on their own they are called *reflexive pronouns*; a reflexive pronoun refers to a noun or another pronoun and indicates that the same person or thing is involved. For example, the sentence "We bought this hockey equipment ourselves" contains the reflexive pronoun "ourselves."

Identify the errors in the following sentence and correct them.

Shirley, itself, will take care of finding a new place to practice.

This sentence contains an error in the use of the intensive pronoun. An intensive pronoun must agree with the noun that it is modifying. In this case, the intensive pronoun must agree with "Shirley," but "itself" refers to an object or thing and not a person. The correct pronoun form would be "herself" because it is a female-gender singular pronoun. So the sentence should read: "Shirley, herself, will take care of finding a new place to practice." In the sentence, the pronoun is used to create a sense of emphasis. This pronoun usage is different from a reflexive pronoun. Instead of emphasizing a noun or pronoun, a reflexive pronoun refers back to a noun or pronoun.

Identify the errors in the following sentence and correct them.

Tennis is thought to have their origins in the Orient.

This sentence contains an incorrect possessive pronoun. While "their" is supposed to refer to "tennis" as its antecedent, it does not agree with that noun either in number or person. Tennis is the name of a game. It is not a person, so the use of the pronoun "their" is incorrect because it refers to people. Tennis is also a singular noun so it does not agree with the plural possessive pronoun "their." The sentence needs to be corrected so that the possessive pronoun is singular and agrees with the noun "tennis." The correct possessive pronoun is "its." The revised sentence should read, "Tennis is thought to have its origins in the Orient."

REWRITE THE FOLLOWING SENTENCE TO MAKE IT CLEARER WHAT THE PRONOUN "IT" REFERS TO.

If you leave your notebook in your backpack, you will forget it.

What does the sentence mean? It is unclear in the sentence whether "it" refers to "notebook" or "backpack." The sentence could be interpreted in either way. The problem is that there is no clear antecedent, so the sentence must be rewritten to make the writer's intention evident. The best way to write the sentence to correct the error is, "You will forget your notebook if you leave it in your backpack." That way, "it" clearly refers to "notebook" and not "backpack," making the meaning of the sentence obvious. When you write, make sure that all pronouns clearly refer to the noun or pronoun intended. They should also agree in number and person.

IDENTIFY THE ERRORS IN THE FOLLOWING SENTENCES AND CORRECT THEM.

Many who learn the trombone may have his difficulties at first. Each of the musical instruments presents their own challenge.

Both sentences contain an incorrect pronoun. In the first sentence, the possessive pronoun "his" does not agree with the plural indefinite pronoun "many." "Many" takes a plural possessive form, so the first sentence should read, "Many who learn the trombone may have *their* difficulties." The second sentence has the opposite problem: the indefinite pronoun "each" is singular, so the pronoun that refers to it must be singular as well. The correct possessive form of "each" is "its" because the sentence is talking about a thing and not a person. So the correct way to write the second sentence is, "Each of the musical instruments presents its own challenge." The second sentence is tricky because the plural noun "instruments" might be interpreted as the antecedent, but it is not. "Each" is the subject of the sentence and the antecedent for "its."

COMMAS, PARENTHESES, AND DASHES

Commas, parentheses, and dashes are used to set off nonrestrictive or parenthetical elements in a sentence. They are used to keep the extra information apart from the flow of the sentence. In the following sentence, commas are used to set aside additional information: "The word tycoon comes from a Japanese word, *taikun*, meaning mighty lord, which in turn comes from two Chinese words." In this next sentence, the additional information is set apart by parentheses: "The ruins of ancient Troy are located in Turkey, about four miles (6.4 kilometers) from the mouth of the Dardanelles." Here, parentheses are used to set off the additional information that the writer wanted to include without making it a formal part of the sentence. Generally, it is best to use parentheses when including dates or data about someone or something. Finally, dashes are used in the following sentence to set information apart: "The circus performer was sitting calmly in a chair—fifty feet above the crowd—while waving a flag."

IDENTIFY THE ERRORS IN THE FOLLOWING SENTENCES AND CORRECT THEM.

Most people do not know that the sandwich was named after John Montagu, the fourth Earl of Sandwich 1718-1782.

During the reign of Elizabeth I, England by defeating the Spanish Armada in 1588 became a great sea power.

The best way to separate the extra information in the first sentence from the rest of the sentence is by using parentheses, which are commonly used to separate dates or data. This would make the sentence both clearer and grammatically correct, which it is not at the present moment. The sentence should read: "Most people do not know that the sandwich was named after John Montagu, the fourth Earl of Sandwich (1718-1782)." Be sure to put the period after the closing parenthesis and not before it. The second sentence has information that is an aside, and needs to be separated from the main sentence. Either commas or dashes would work. So the sentence could be written: "During the reign of Elizabeth I, England, by defeating the Spanish Armada in 1588, became a great sea power." Or it could be: "During the reign of Elizabeth I, England—by defeating the Spanish Armada in 1588—became a great sea power.

WHICH WORDS ARE MISSPELLED IN THE FOLLOWING SENTENCE?

> She hoped that the lectore would benifit her understanding of fine litarature.

The words that are misspelled are "lectore," "benifit," and "litarature," which are spelled "lecture," "benefit," and "literature" respectively. It is important to learn to spell words correctly. There are certain skills you can use to help you spell words correctly. Sounding out words is one of them. Breaking longer words down into syllables, affixes, and roots can help you figure out the way a word should be spelled. Making a list of new words is a good habit to get into, and using those words in sentences will help you remember them. Also, use the basic spelling rules, such as "I before E except after C," (believe) as well as "drop the final e" (take, taking) and "double the last consonant" (hop, hopping).

CONTEXT CLUES

Context clues are the clues that are contained in the sentence or sentences around an unknown word. A reader can often figure out the meaning of an unknown word from these clues. For instance, a passage might say that John and Stan had absolute trust in each other's decisions. A reader might not be familiar with the word "absolute," but then the passage goes on to say that John and Stan really believed in each other and always accepted each other's decisions. These facts give clues about the meaning of "absolute." The reader could conclude that "absolute" means "total" or "complete." Another helpful clue is that the word "absolute" comes before a noun, "trust," so it is logical to think that it is an adjective. This tells the reader that the word and any synonyms for it must also be adjectives.

USING CONTEXT CLUES, DETERMINE THE MEANING OF "SPECIALIZES" IN THE FOLLOWING EXCERPT.

> Charley is a great salesman. He can sell books and beds and towels and washing machines. He can sell anything. But Charley specializes in selling carpets. That is all he sells now.

You can figure out from the excerpt that the word "specializes" means "concentrates"—doing one thing. The context clues tell you this is the word's meaning. The excerpt says that Charley is a great salesman and that he can sell books, beds, towels and washing machines. In fact, the excerpt says he can sell anything, but it ends by saying that he only sells carpets now—he *specializes* in that. If you substitute the words "concentrates on" for "specializes in," the sentence makes sense. He is only selling carpets now. Both words are verbs, so that helps to let you know that this is probably the correct choice of synonym.

AFFIXES AND ROOTS

A *root word* is a word that can be added onto. An *affix* is a prefix or suffix that is added onto a root word. Often, the affixes in the English language come from Latin or Greek origins. A *prefix* is added to the beginning of a root word and a *suffix* is added to the end of a root word. When you look at the meaning of a root word and the meaning of any affixes added to the root word, you can figure out the approximate meaning of the word. For example, the root word "happy" means "to be content." The prefix "un-" means "not." The reader can therefore figure out that "unhappy" means to "not being content."

Figuring Out the Meaning of the Word "Misconception" Based on Its Root and Affixes

The word "misconception" is made up of three sections: a root, a prefix, and a suffix. To figure out the meaning of the word, you need to analyze these parts of the word individually. The root "concept" means "idea." It comes from the Latin word *conceptus* meaning "something conceived. There are two affixes in the word. The prefix *mis-* means "not" or "bad." The suffix *-tion* means "action" or "process." Put these meanings together and the word "misconception" means "the act of having a bad idea" or "misunderstanding." Studying roots and affixes is important because it allows you to decode words that you might not otherwise understand with relative ease.

Using Specialized Reference Materials to Determine the Pronunciation of a Word

A print or digital dictionary can be used as a means to find the correct pronunciation of words. The dictionary will have a guide that shows how to sound out the words, the symbols used to indicate the sounds, along with sample sounds (like the "i" in "pie," for instance). The dictionary can also be used to determine the meaning of the word, as well as its part of speech. The thesaurus is useful because it lists synonyms for all the various meanings a word can have, which helps to clarify the precise meaning as used in the context of the text you are reading. Many books will have a glossary placed at the end of the book to help you with difficult or unfamiliar words used in the text.

Julia used her dictionary to check the various meanings of the word "clear." She found this entry:

clear (klîr) adj. 1.obvious. 2. easily seen through. 3. free from flaw or blemish. 4. free from guilt; untroubled 5. out of the way. v. int. 6. to tidy. 7. to free 8. To earn.

Identify which definition of "clear" is used in the following sentence:

Janet stood clear of the crowd pushing to get through the door.

The correct answer is meaning 5: "out of the way." If you substitute that definition for the word, the sentence makes sense. Meanings 1, 2, 3, and 4 do not fit with the context of the sentence. Meanings 6, 7, and 8 are verbs and "clear" as it is used in the sample is an adjective. When considering which meaning is being used, always check for context clues in the sentence or in the sentences before or after the sentence in which the word is used. Dictionaries also tell you how to pronounce words and often the derivation of the word, although that is not given here.

Discuss the meaning of the word "steep" in the following sentence.

The price of the designer shoes was too steep for Stephanie to even consider buying them.

The word "steep" can mean many things. In this instance, it means "expensive." The context of the sentence helps the reader figure this out because the sentence says that Stephanie would not even consider buying the shoes because the price was too "steep." If you substitute the word "expensive" for "steep," the sentence continues to make sense. This is a good way to determine if you have the correct meaning of a word. The other meanings of the word "steep" do not fit in the sentence. To figure out the meaning of the word, use the context clues and then check the meaning of the word in a dictionary. A dictionary will also help determine the meaning of the word by saying what part of speech it is when used in a particular instance. In this case the word "steep" is used as an adjective.

Explain what figure of speech is used in the following sentence.

The wind called out to the lost pioneers, warning them to take shelter.

This is an example of personification, one of many different figures of speech. *Personification* is the act of giving human traits to things. Here the wind is "calling out" and "warning" the pioneers. Wind does not really call out or warn people. It may seem as though it does, but only people can call out or warn people. Other kinds of figures of speech or figurative language include *similes*, which uses the words "like" and "as" to compare two things to each other; *metaphors*, where two things are compared without using comparison words; and *hyperbole*, an exaggeration meant to create an impression without being taken literally.

Using the Relationships Between Words to Better Understand Them

You can use the relationships between words to better understand them. Some words indicate a cause and effect relationship. These include "as a result," "because," "since" and "consequently," to name a few. When you see these words, you will know that a cause and effect relationship exists, which may help you understand how the words relate to one another. Other relationship words include "part" and "whole" and "item" and "category." A whole is made up of parts, and a category is made up of items. If you see the word "part," look for the word that is the whole. If you see the word "item," look for the word that is the category. In this way you will better understand these terms.

Connotations vs. Denotations of Words

The *denotation* of a word is what the dictionary definition of that word is. The *connotation* of a word is what the word suggests beyond its dictionary meaning. It is both the meaning that is associated with that word and a subjective interpretation of the word's meaning. The denotation meaning is objective. For instance, the words "stingy" and "thrifty" basically mean not being wasteful. However, "stingy" carries with it the connotation of being thrifty to such an extent as to be seen as being miserly; it is not a positive term. "Thrifty" can be seen as a virtue, while "stingy" is not. When you read, you should pay particular attention to the language that a writer uses to describe something. Look for words that suggest something about a place or person that are not directly stated in the text.

Determine the difference in the connotations between the words "doting" and "affectionate."

The word "doting" is a term that is used to convey a negative connotation in that it means caring about someone excessively, to the point of overlooking the reality of the person. "Affectionate," on the other hand, has a more positive connotation of someone who simply cares for someone else very much. "Doting" is a much more extreme word. It suggests a lot about a person who is described as doting, as though the person would overlook any wrongdoing by the person that is being cared for. "Affectionate" does not have that extreme meaning; it is more benign.

Improving Comprehension

It is important to acquire and accurately use words and phrases at the appropriate level so as to improve comprehension and expression. Such a skill helps the student to perform well in the classroom as well as on standardized testing. A student who does not read at the appropriate level will have to continually stop while reading so he or she can look up the meaning of words. Someone who does not have a good vocabulary will take a great deal longer to comprehend new material in class as well as information that may be encountered in life. Students should make an attempt to develop their vocabulary by keeping lists of new words and using them in sentences. Students should be very familiar with dictionary use as well as thesaurus use. Having a good vocabulary is valuable not only for reading well, but also for writing well. It is important, too, to be able to express what you mean precisely and for that you need to improve your vocabulary.

English Language Arts/Literacy Practice Test #1

Practice Questions

Questions 1 – 8 pertain to the following short story:

A World of White: The Iditarod Trail

(1) Imagine clinging desperately to your sled as brutal winds batter your body. The path ahead appears and disappears like a mirage, frequently obscured by blowing curtains of snow. You are freezing and sweating at the same time. Your throat burns with thirst, and your body aches with fatigue. You know your dogs must feel it too, so you encourage them to press on to the next checkpoint. All around you, the world is endless, empty, and white. Welcome to the Iditarod Trail.

(2) Alaska's Iditarod Trail is the world's most famous sled dog racing venue. But the trail is older than the sport of sled dog racing. In fact, the Iditarod Trail was first established in the early 1900s, during the Alaskan gold rush. In those days, dog teams were used for work, hauling thousands of pounds of gold from landlocked Iditarod to the port of Anchorage. But in faraway Nome, also known for gold, six-year-old George Allen had the idea to put together a race to see whose sled dogs were fastest, and the sport of sled dog racing was born.

(3) Though the Iditarod Trail race is the most famous race in the sport of sled dog racing, the first race along the trail was actually a race to save lives. In 1925, a diphtheria outbreak began in Nome. To prevent an epidemic that could kill thousands, doctors were desperate for the vaccine serum, but the closest serum was in Anchorage. The train ran from Anchorage to the village of Nenana, but that was still 674 miles from Nome. A cry for help was sent by the doctors, and in the midst of the blizzards and windstorms of January, the call was answered. Twenty brave mushers drove their dogs in a frantic relay, carrying 300,000 bottles of serum from Nenana to Nome. They followed the Iditarod Trail.

(4) Dog sledding, or "mushing," became quite popular after that heroic journey, but by the 1960s, it had lost popularity and the Iditarod Trail had been largely forgotten. There were a few lovers of mushing, however, who worked tirelessly to reestablish the Iditarod Trail and create a new sled dog race that used the trail as its course. The first official race was held in 1967 to celebrate the centennial of the purchase of Alaska from Russia. The race involved 58 drivers who mushed 56 miles in two days. This race was a success, but the popularity and future of the Iditarod Trail was still in question.

(5) In March of 1973, the first Anchorage to Nome Iditarod Trail race was organized and held. This race was much longer than previous races, covering more than 1,000 miles—the whole Iditarod Trail. Thirty-four mushers began the race, but only 22 were able to finish. After the 1973 race, the popularity of the Iditarod Trail finally grew and was firmly established. In 1978, the Iditarod Trail became a National Historic Trail.

(6) The modern Iditarod Trail race is open to mushers over 18 years old who have qualified in a recognized race of 200 miles or more. For younger mushers between 14 and 18 years old, the Junior Iditarod offers a 130-mile version of the race. Many Junior Iditarod participants go on to compete in the Iditarod Trail race, as the Junior Iditarod is good practice for the grueling trek of the main race. All mushers must prepare for the race extensively, often for months before the race. Many mushers run their dogs more than 1,500 miles in preparation, giving them experience in all types of weather and terrain.

(7) To enter the Iditarod Trail race, participants must pay an entrance fee. Then they must travel to Anchorage with their dogs. In Anchorage, they attend a mushers' banquet where they are given their racing order numbers. Afterwards, all participating dogs are checked by a veterinarian and marked by race officials to prevent dog switching mid-race, which is not allowed. The dogs are even drug tested at the beginning and at checkpoints throughout the race to prevent cheating! Finally, the sleds and equipment are checked. Then participants are ready to start the race.

(8) On the morning of the Iditarod Trail race, mushers leave Anchorage in their assigned racing order. They are sent out one at a time, at two-minute intervals. For more than a week—sometimes up to three weeks—they travel throughout Alaska, stopping at designated checkpoints all along the Iditarod Trail as they make their way to Nome. When all participants have reached Nome, another mushers' banquet is held. Awards are given, and everyone is applauded for their achievement. Win or lose, the mushers know that only the toughest of the tough have what it takes to finish the race and conquer the great Iditarod Trail.

1. What does the simile in paragraph 1 describe?

a. The snow
b. The path
c. The musher's throat
d. The dogs

This question has two parts. Answer Part A then answer Part B.

2. Part A: What is the best description of the word "diphtheria" in paragraph 3?

a. a mode of transportation
b. an illness
c. a trail name
d. a celebration

Part B: Which sentence from the passage best supports your answer from Part A?

____

____

____

3. What two cities are on the ends of the Iditarod Trail?

a. Anchorage and Nome
b. Nome and Nenana
c. Iditarod and Anchorage
d. Nenana and Iditarod

4. What is the author's main purpose in writing this article?

a. To encourage mushers to race on the Iditarod Trail
b. To inform the reader about the 1925 diphtheria outbreak
c. To describe the terrain of Alaska
d. To educate the reader about the Iditarod Trail

5. In paragraph 3, which words best convey the feelings of the doctors in Nome in 1925?

a. "Epidemic" and "diphtheria"
b. "Blizzards" and "windstorms"
c. "Brave" and "frantic relay"
d. "Desperate" and "cry for help"

6. Why did the author choose to write this article in third-person point of view?

a. Historical overviews are best written in third person
b. The author has never been to Alaska
c. Third person is the required point of view in nonfiction writing
d. This article is not written in third-person point of view

7. How is this article organized?

a. Chronologically
b. Geographically
c. Randomly
d. Spatially

This question has two parts. Answer Part A then answer Part B.

8. Part A: Which sentence is a main idea?

a. To prevent an epidemic that could kill thousands, doctors were desperate for the vaccine serum, but the closest serum was in Anchorage.
b. Alaska's Iditarod Trail is the world's most famous sled dog racing venue
c. Thirty-four mushers began the race, but only 22 were able to finish.
d. For more than a week—sometimes up to three weeks—they travel throughout Alaska, stopping at designated checkpoints all along the Iditarod Trail as they make their way to Nome.

Part B: Based on your answer in Part A. Which of the following is a supporting detail in this article?

a. Alaska's Iditarod Trail is the world's most famous sled dog racing venue
b. After the heroic journey of 1925, mushing became more popular
c. In fact, the Iditarod Trail was first established in the early 1900s, during the Alaskan gold rush
d. There are specific requirements to enter the Iditarod Trail race

Questions 9 –17pertain to the following story:

The Right Thing to Do

Characters *(in order of appearance)*:

JESSICA—a sixth-grade girl, Amy's friend

GROUP OF FRIENDS—a group of sixth-grade girls

AMY—a sixth-grade girl, Jessica's friend

SALES CLERK—a clerk in the store Amy and Jessica visit

Scene 1

(1) *Jessica stands with a group of friends on the school steps. The group is chatting and laughing. Amy approaches from stage right.*

(2) AMY: Jessica! Jessica!

(3) JESSICA: *(turning away from her friends and taking a step toward Amy)* Hi, Amy. What's up?

(4) AMY: I'm headed to the mall, and I thought you might want to come.

(5) JESSICA: Why me? I thought we weren't friends anymore.

(6) AMY: *(waving her hand and shaking her head)* That old fight? Ancient history. So ... do you want to come or not?

(7) JESSICA: *(glancing back at her friends)* Sure. I'll come. Just give me a minute.

(8) *Jessica runs back and talks with her friends for a moment, then rejoins Amy. Amy and Jessica exit stage right.*

Scene 2

(9) *Amy and Jessica are looking at a shelf full of lipstick in a cosmetics store in the mall.*

(10) AMY: Look at this one, Jess. Don't you just love this color? *(She picks up a lipstick tube.)*

(11) JESSICA: It's nice, but I like this one better. *(She picks up a different tube of lipstick.)*

(12) *A sales clerk enters from stage left.*

(13) SALES CLERK: *(stopping by the girls)* Can I help you ladies find something?

(14) AMY: Oh, no. We're just looking.

(15) JESSICA: Thank you, though.

(16) SALES CLERK: Okay. Well, let me know if you need anything. *(He/she exits stage right.)*

(17) AMY: So, which one are you going to get?

(18) JESSICA: *(looking at the floor and shaking her head)* I'm not getting one. They're a little spendy for me. Besides, I'm saving up for something special.

(19) AMY: *(laughing)* Who said anything about money? *(She slips her favorite lipstick into her pocket.)* I didn't ask you which one you were going to buy. I asked which one you were going to get. So, which one will it be?

(20) JESSICA: But—but—that's stealing!

(21) AMY: Look at all these tubes of lipstick. They'll never miss a couple.

(22) JESSICA: *(looking around nervously)* What if that sales clerk comes back and catches us?

(23) AMY: You worry too much. *(She picks up two tubes of lipstick.)* Now, was this the one you liked? Or was it this one? Never mind. We'll take them both. *(She slips them both into her pocket.)*

(24) JESSICA: Amy! This is wrong. We shouldn't be doing this.

(25) AMY: *(glaring at Jessica)* Do you even want to be my friend again? It sure doesn't sound like it.

(26) JESSICA: Of course I want to be your friend. It's just—

(27) AMY: Then come on. Let's go. *(She starts to walk away, and then turns and looks back.)* Are you coming?

(28) JESSICA: Fine. *(She follows Amy.)* But what if the alarm goes off?

(29) AMY: For a couple of tubes of lipstick? Not gonna happen. Now, follow me. And for heaven's sake, don't look so nervous.

(30) *The girls exit stage right.*

Scene 3

(31) *Jessica reenters the cosmetics store from stage right. She stops at the shelf of lipsticks and looks around. The sales clerk enters from stage left.*

(32) JESSICA: Excuse me ...

(33) SALES CLERK: *(stopping)* Did you need help with something?

(34) JESSICA: Yes. *(She looks at the floor.)* My friend who was just with me, um, she took—well, actually, she stole three tubes of lipstick. I'm not okay with that. So, um, I wanted to pay for them.

(35) SALES CLERK: That's impressive. I've never seen that happen before. And kids take stuff from this store all the time. What made you come back?

(36) JESSICA: *(shrugging)* I don't know. I guess it was just the right thing to do.

This question has two parts. Answer Part A then answer Part B.

9. Part A: In paragraph 6, what does Amy mean when she calls her fight with Jessica "ancient history"?

a. It happened thousands of years ago
b. It happened in history class
c. Amy has totally forgotten about the fight
d. They were arguing about events in ancient history

Part B: Which sentence supports your answer from Part A?

a. That old fight?
b. Sure. I'll come.
c. I'm headed to the mall, and I thought you might want to come.
d. *Jessica runs back and talks with her friends for a moment, then rejoins Amy.*

10. What is the setting for Scene 1?

a. The school steps
b. The mall
c. A cosmetics store
d. Amy's house

11. What is the setting for Scene 2 and Scene 3?

a. The school steps
b. Jessica's house
c. A cosmetics store
d. Amy's house

12. Which scene contains the climax of this play?

a. Scene 1
b. Scene 2
c. Scene 3
d. All of the above

13. Which scene contains the denouement of this play?

a. Scene 1
b. Scene 2
c. Scene 3
d. All of the above

14. In paragraph 6, what type of figurative language is used when Amy says "ancient history"?

a. Metaphor
b. Simile
c. Personification
d. Hyperbole

15. Which of the following best describes the overall tone of this play?

a. Formal
b. Conversational
c. Classical
d. Musical

16. What is the underlying theme of this play?

a. Amy and Jessica are best friends
b. Doing the right thing is always a good decision
c. It is okay to steal if you are not caught
d. Shopping for cosmetics increases peer pressure

17. Which paragraph best shows Amy's justification for stealing the lipstick?

a. Paragraph 21
b. Paragraph 23
c. Paragraph 25
d. Paragraph 29

Questions 18– 29 pertain to the following two short stories:

THE TALENT SHOW

(1) The first notes floated from the piano. Megan smiled, warm and excited beneath the glaring stage lights. This was her moment. She had practiced. She had prepared. She was ready. As the introduction ended, Megan opened her mouth and began to sing.

(2) The song flowed along, and Megan relaxed, scanning the faces of the audience. But somewhere in the middle of the second verse, her mind suddenly went blank. The music went on, but the words were gone. Megan's smile faded. She stood silently with her mouth hanging open. When the music finally trickled to a stop, Megan ran from the stage.

(3) In a cramped dressing room backstage, Megan buried her face in her hands. She had wanted so much to win this talent show. Tears seeped between her fingers. Her confidence and pride and excitement had been replaced by utter disappointment. She felt a hand on her shoulder and lifted her damp face.

(4) "Ella and Kaylee are here," Megan's mom said, giving her shoulder a quick squeeze.

(5) Ella and Kaylee, Megan's two best friends, pulled folding chairs over to face Megan. She looked at them forlornly.

(6) "I'm a total failure," she moaned.

(7) Ella and Kaylee exchanged glances. Kaylee reached out and squeezed Megan's hand.

(8) "What are you talking about?" Kaylee said. "That first verse was some of your best singing ever."

(9) "Thanks," Megan said. "But the problem is that the first verse is all I sang. Then I totally bombed. I can't believe I forgot the words after all that practice."

(10) "You didn't totally bomb," Ella said. "You just forgot the words. That happens to everybody. Besides, don't the pros say you should leave your audience wanting more?"

(11) "I guess so," Megan admitted.

(12) "Well, trust me," Ella said. "I guarantee they wanted more—like the rest of the song! You probably did, too."

(13) Megan smiled a little. "So, you guys don't think I'm a total dork for forgetting the words?"

(14) "Of course not," Kaylee said. "Forgetting the words doesn't make you a dork. It just makes you human. And you're still the most talented person I know."

(15) Ella nodded in agreement. Megan pulled Ella and Kaylee into a quick hug. Then she wiped her eyes and managed a genuine smile.

(16) "I'm so lucky to have best friends like you two," Megan said. "It's nice to know that you'll be my friends forever, no matter what!"

The Tournament

(1) Looking for a hole in the defense, Scott dribbled the ball, shifting it from hand to hand. A trickle of sweat ran down his back. No one was open. There were only seconds left on the clock, and Scott knew he had a difficult decision to make.

(2) The other team was leading by two points, and Scott was just outside the three-point line. If he could make the shot, the Eagles would be state champions again. But if he missed ... Scott didn't want to think about that. He knew what he had to do.

(3) It was a classic jump shot. The ball left his hands and sailed toward the basket in a perfect arc. The crowd, the other players, the whole stadium seemed frozen in time. All eyes were on the ball as it struck the rim and bounced off. The buzzer blared. The game was over. Scott had missed, and the Eagles had lost.

(4) Scott stood like a statue on the court as people surged around him. Elated family members swarmed the winning team. Teammates hugged and slapped each other on the back. Even Scott's own teammates joined in the celebration.

(5) Suddenly, Scott felt himself being hoisted unsteadily onto the shoulders of his friends. Over the loudspeaker, the announcer proclaimed that Scott had been named the most valuable player of the championship game. Everyone cheered, and the Eagles took a victory lap with Scott on their shoulders. Finally, Scott's friends put him back on solid ground.

(6) Scott was bewildered. He was the one who missed the most important shot of the game. How could anyone call him the most valuable player? He didn't feel very valuable at the moment. Scott approached Coach Travis.

(7) "Coach," Scott said, "there must be some mistake. I can't be the most valuable player."

(8) "There's no mistake," Coach Travis said. "You had 26 points, 11 rebounds, and 8 assists. I'd say that makes you a very valuable player."

(9) "But I missed that last shot," Scott said. "We lost the game because of me."

(10) "I don't know about that," said Coach Travis. "Everybody misses a shot from time to time. Don't be so hard on yourself. It's all about perspective."

(11) "What do you mean?" Scott asked.

(12) "Well," Coach Travis answered, "you could say you are the reason we lost the game because you missed that last shot. On the other hand, you could say you are the reason we almost won because of your awesome performance throughout the game. How you look at it is up to you."

(13) Scott's teammates came running over and surrounded Coach Travis. They jostled one another playfully, talking and laughing.

(14) "Hey, Coach," one player called out, "how about treating your team to pizza?"

(15) "I don't know," said Coach Travis. "Do you think you deserve pizza?"

(16) Scott piped up. "Of course we do! After all, we almost won the game."

(17) Coach Travis smiled. "You're right, Scott. We did almost win. Okay. Pizza for everyone!"

Questions 18-22 pertain to "The Talent Show" short story:

18. Which of the following is the best definition of "forlornly" as it is used in paragraph 5?

a. With a happy spirit
b. With a sad spirit
c. With a lonely spirit
d. With an angry spirit

19. What is the main theme of this story?

a. Real friends support you, no matter what
b. It is easy to forget the words of a song
c. Performing in a talent show can be embarrassing
d. Megan feels like a failure

20. What point of view is used to tell this story?

a. First person
b. Second person
c. Third person
d. None of the above

21. Which of the following is a supporting detail in this story?

a. Megan is singing in a talent show
b. Megan forgets the words of her song
c. Megan is disappointed in herself
d. Megan is accompanied by piano music

22. What does Kaylee do in paragraph 8 to try to make Megan feel better?

a. She makes a joke about Megan's performance
b. She compliments Megan on her singing
c. She tells about a time when she forgot a song
d. She sings a song with Megan

Questions 23-27 pertain to "The Tournament" short story:

23. In paragraph 4, what does "elated" mean?

a. Happy and excited
b. Frustrated and angry
c. Loud and rowdy
d. Pushy and proud

24. In the first sentence of paragraph 4, what type of figurative language is used?

a. Hyperbole
b. Metaphor
c. Personification
d. Simile

25. Which of the following best expresses the theme of this story?

a. The Eagles want to be the state champions
b. There are different ways to look at any situation
c. Winning isn't everything
d. Scott is a very good basketball player

26. Which of the following is the best summary of this story?

a. At the buzzer, Scott misses an important basket because he isn't a very good basketball player
b. Coach Travis feels Scott is the most valuable player in the game because he scored 26 points
c. When Scott misses an important shot, he is disappointed, but Coach Travis shows him there are different ways to look at the situation
d. The Eagles lose the state championship because of Scott, but Coach Travis sees things differently and makes Scott the most valuable player

27. Why is Scott so upset in this story?

a. He feels responsible for losing the game
b. He thinks he is a bad basketball player
c. He doesn't like Coach Travis
d. He doesn't want to play basketball anymore

Questions 28-29 pertain to both "The Talent Show" and "The Tournament" short stories:

28. In what ways are Scott and Megan most similar in these stories?

a. They are both performers.
b. They are both very active.
c. They are both disappointed in themselves.
d. They both have good friends.

This question has two parts. Answer Part A then answer Part B.

29. Part A: What general theme is evident in both stories?

a. Winning is important, but it isn't everything
b. Good friends are the most valuable thing in life
c. Coaches can offer good perspective on tough situations
d. When you try your best, you shouldn't be disappointed in yourself

Part B: Write down a sentence or sentences from each story that proves this is true.

___

___

___

___

___

Questions 30-40 pertain to the following story:

Everybody's Problem

(1) I used to think homeless people were dirty and lazy and mean. I thought they were all old men with scraggly beards and mangy dogs. I thought they lived on the street because they wanted to. I thought they were all drug addicts and alcoholics who ate from garbage cans and slept in boxes. I used to think homelessness wasn't my problem. Then I met Chris, and he showed me I was wrong—about everything. Homelessness is everybody's problem.

(2) The sun was climbing into the bright blue sky as we loaded up the bus at the youth center. It was a crisp, cold Thanksgiving morning, and our youth group was headed down to a local shelter called The Lighthouse. We were going to serve Thanksgiving dinner to more than a hundred homeless people. It seemed like an appropriate way to spend Thanksgiving Day.

(3) When we arrived at the shelter, we were each given a job to do. My job was peeling potatoes. The shelter director gave me a peeler and a garbage can and sat me down in front of a giant pile of potatoes. I had never seen so many potatoes in one place before. They rose from the tray like Mt. Everest. By the time I had peeled them all, my hands and arms and shoulders ached.

(4) When the kitchen work was done, we were given our serving stations. The director explained that this was the only meal many of the homeless people would eat that day, and for some, it was the only hot meal they would have that week. Even

so, there wasn't a lot of food for so many people. We were supposed to give each person one slice of turkey, one scoop of mashed potatoes, one scoop of stuffing, a small drizzle of gravy, a few green beans, and a sliver of pumpkin pie.

(5) I was plodding along, dishing up mashed potatoes with an ice cream scoop, when I happened to look up at the person I was serving. He wasn't a dirty, bearded old man. He was a boy about my age, with brown hair and brown eyes and a patched green jacket.

(6) "Hi," the boy said. "I'm Chris."

(7) "I'm Ben," I said as I scooped some potatoes onto his plate. "Happy Thanksgiving."

(8) "Thanks," Chris said, and then he was gone.

(9) As Chris moved down the line, I began to look around, really seeing things for the first time. Very few of the homeless people fit my stereotype. There were men and women, old and young. Children played in a corner of the dining room. At one table, teenagers talked in a tight group. People chatted and smiled. A few were even laughing. This was not what I had pictured a homeless shelter would be like.

(10) When everyone had been served, I began to help clean up. I couldn't help watching Chris as I cleared the tables and wiped them down. He was playing peek-a-boo with a little girl in a high chair. I wondered if it was his little sister.

(11) I was so lost in thought that I jumped when the shelter director tapped my shoulder. She laughed.

(12) "I'll finish cleaning up here," she said. "Why don't you go talk to Chris? He's very nice."

(13) As I approached the table where Chris was sitting, I felt nervous. What would I say? Could we possibly have anything to talk about? Would he even want to talk to me? I sat cautiously beside him.

(14) "Hi, Ben," he said.

(15) "Hi, Chris. Is that your little sister?"

(16) Chris smiled. "Yep. This is Sophia. And over there is my little brother, Dane." Chris motioned toward the corner where the smaller children were playing. Then he pointed to a dark-haired woman at a nearby table. "That's my mom."

(17) "Are you all homeless?" I asked.

(18) "Yep," answered Chris. "We've been here at The Lighthouse for almost two months now. It's okay here, but I miss my old school and my friends. I hope we can move back to a real house soon."

(19) "I didn't know there was such a thing as homeless kids," I admitted.

(20) "Me neither," said Chris. "At least, not until I became one."

(21) "How did it happen?" I asked. Then I had second thoughts. "I mean, you don't have to tell me if you don't want to. I was just wondering."

(22) "It's okay," Chris said. "I don't mind talking about it. About a year ago, my dad got really sick. He was in the hospital for a few months. Then he died. We didn't have any insurance or anything, and my mom couldn't get a job. Besides, she was really sad, and she was trying to take care of me and Dane and Sophia."

(23) "So, how did you end up homeless?" I wondered.

(24) "Mom says there were just too many bills and not enough money. First, we got our lights turned off. Then we couldn't pay our rent, so we had to move out of our house. We stayed with friends for a while, but eventually there was nobody left to stay with. So, we came here."

(25) "Will you stay here forever?" I asked.

(26) "No," Chris said. "My mom is in a program to give her training and help her get a job. When she finds a job, we can get a new place to live. Then things can be normal again."

(27) I heard my youth leader calling for us to load the bus. I wanted to talk to Chris more and ask him more questions, but I knew I had to leave. I stood up.

(28) "I have to go," I said. "I'm glad I got to meet you, Chris. I hope you get a new house soon."

(29) "Thanks, Ben," Chris said. "It was nice to meet you, too. Thanks for hanging out with me for a while. Happy Thanksgiving."

(30) "Happy Thanksgiving," I echoed as I headed toward the door. When I looked back, Chris waved. Then he started playing peek-a-boo with Sophia again.

(31) I will probably never see Chris again, but I have thought of him many times since that day. In just a few minutes together, he taught me so much about the problem of homelessness. It isn't just a problem that affects lazy, mean old men. It affects men and women of all ages. It affects children. It affects whole families. It affected Chris. And because I got the chance to see homelessness through his eyes, it affects me now, too. I think I'll go back again next Thanksgiving ... or maybe sooner. After all, now I know that homelessness is everybody's problem.

30. What is the setting for this story?

a. A youth center
b. A homeless shelter
c. A community center
d. A school

31. If you were describing this story, what classification would you use?

a. Memoir
b. Biography
c. Autobiography
d. Fiction

32. In paragraph 9, what does the word "stereotype" mean?

a. A textbook definition of a concept
b. Height, weight, and physical features
c. A generalized idea of what something is like
d. A description given by an authority figure

33. What point of view is used to tell this story?

a. First person
b. Second person
c. Third person
d. All of the above

34. What is the main theme of this story?

a. Kids can be homeless
b. Potatoes are difficult to peel
c. Serving at a homeless shelter is a good Thanksgiving project
d. Homelessness is everybody's problem

This question has two parts. Answer Part A then answer Part B.

35. Part A: What does the author compare the potatoes to in paragraph 3?

a. A tower
b. A mountain range
c. Mt. Everest
d. A mound

Part B: Based on your answer in Part A why does he make that comparison?

a. They were the biggest potatoes he had ever seen.
b. The potatoes were shaped like mountains.
c. The potatoes were piled really high.
d. He just likes Mt. Everest.

36. Which of the following items was not included in the Thanksgiving dinner at the shelter?

a. Turkey
b. Cranberry sauce
c. Mashed potatoes and gravy
d. Pumpkin pie

37. What major event in the life of Chris's family led to their homelessness?

a. Their house burned down
b. Chris's mom lost her job
c. They had to live in their car
d. Chris's dad got sick and died

This question has two parts. Answer Part A then answer Part B.

38. Part A: What do you think the author's primary purpose was in telling this story?

a. To persuade the reader to do something about homelessness
b. To inform the reader about The Lighthouse homeless shelter
c. To educate the reader on Thanksgiving service projects
d. To entertain the reader with a story about a personal experience

Part B: Which paragraph from the story best supports your answer in Part A?

a. Paragraph 3
b. Paragraph 6
c. Paragraph 5
d. Paragraph 1

39. Which of the following is the best summary of this story?

a. In the beginning, Ben hates homeless people, but at the end, he loves them
b. Ben goes to a homeless shelter to serve Thanksgiving dinner and learns that homelessness affects everyone
c. The Lighthouse is a wonderful shelter that serves individuals and families who are homeless
d. Ben peels potatoes, serves food, meets Chris, and then goes home

40. Which of the following is Ben most likely to do in the future as a result of meeting Chris at The Lighthouse?

a. Avoid homeless people
b. Give away all his money
c. Try living on the street
d. Serve at a homeless shelter again

Answers and Explanations

1. B: A simile compares one thing to another by using "like" or "as"; the only simile in paragraph 1—"like a mirage"—refers to the path.

2. Part A: B: "Diphtheria" is a type of respiratory illness.

Part B: This sentence best supports the answer from Part A: "To prevent an epidemic that could kill thousands, doctors were desperate for the vaccine serum, but the closest serum was in Anchorage." It talks about needing a vaccine which is used to cure illnesses.

3. A: This information is found in Paragraph 5: "In March of 1973, the first Anchorage to Nome Iditarod Trail race was organized and held. This race was much longer than previous races, covering more than 1,000 miles—the whole Iditarod Trail."

4. D: This is an informational article – the author's main purpose in writing this article is to educate the reader about the Iditarod Trail.

5. D: The descriptive word "desperate" and the descriptive phrase "cry for help" are used in reference to the doctors in Nome in 1925.

6. A: Historical overviews, like this one, are best written in the third-person point of view.

7. A: This article is organized chronologically, from earliest to latest dates.

8. Part A: B: This is the only sentence that gives a main idea. All of the other choices are just supporting details.

Part B: C: is a supporting detail that expands on a main idea from the article. A, B, and D are not the best choices because they are all main points in the article instead of supporting details.

9. Part A: C: The phrase "ancient history" is a figure of speech. Amy uses it to communicate that she has totally forgotten about the fight.

Part B: A: Amy refers to it as "that old fight", which shows that it happened a while back and she has already forgotten about it.

10. A: Scene 1 is set on the school steps.

11. C: Scene 2 and Scene 3 take place in a cosmetics store.

12. B: Scene 2 contains the climax of the play, when Jessica must decide whether to go along with Amy or not. In a story, the climax is the most exciting part of the story, when the action or tension builds to a zenith. This occurred when Jessica learned that Amy was planning on stealing the lipstick.

13. C: Scene 3 contains the denouement of the play, when Jessica returns to the store to do the right thing. This is also known as the resolution of the story.

14. D: The use of "ancient history" in paragraph 6 is a hyperbole, a major exaggeration.

15. B: The tone of this play is conversational.

16. B: The underlying theme of the play is that you should always do the right thing, even when it's difficult. This could also be called the moral of the story.

17. A: In Paragraph 21, Amy tries to justify stealing the tubes of lipstick by saying that the store has a lot of them, and stealing only two or three of them won't do any harm because they won't even be missed.

18. B: "Forlornly" is best defined as "with a sad spirit."

19. A most accurately represents the main theme of the story.

20. C: This story is written in the third person. That means the author is writing from the point of view of a narrator – someone who knows all the details of the story but isn't involved in it.

21. D: is only option that offers a supporting detail, while the rest of the answer choices represent important parts of the story.

22. B: In paragraph 8, Kaylee compliments Megan's singing to help her feel better.

23. A: If someone is "elated" , they are extremely happy and excited about something.

24. D: The first sentence of paragraph 4 uses a simile when it says Scott "stood like a statue." A simile uses "like" or "as" to compare one thing to another.

25. B most clearly and completely expresses the theme of the story. Coach Travis tells Scott that "it's all about perspective", and then says that how Scott decides to look at it is up to him.

26. C is the most complete and accurate summary of the story overall. A, B, and D are incorrect because they cover only part of the story or some of the main ideas and concepts.

27. A: Scott is upset in the story because he feels responsible for the team's loss.

28. C: Scott and Megan are most similar in their feelings of disappointment in themselves.

29. Part A: D: clearly reflects a general theme found in both stories.

Part B: An example from *The Talent Show* is, "Forgetting the words doesn't make you a dork. It just makes you human. And you're still the most talented person I know." An example from *The Tournament* is, "Well," Coach Travis answered, "you could say you are the reason we lost the game because you missed that last shot. On the other hand, you could say you are the reason we almost won because of your awesome performance throughout the game. How you look at it is up to you."

30. B: This story is set at a homeless shelter.

31. A: This story is written in the style of a memoir, as evidenced by the first-person, reflective tone.

32. C offers the best definition of "stereotype" as it is used in paragraph 9.

33. A: This story is written in first person. That means the author is involved in the events of the story and is telling it from his point of view.

34. D: The main theme of the story is that homelessness is everybody's problem. One clue that this is the main point of the story is that the author clearly states it in the last line of the story. It's not always true that the last line of a short piece contains the main point, but that is often the case.

35. Part A: C: In paragraph 3 the author uses a simile to compare the size of the pile of potatoes to Mt. Everest.

Part B: In the story he says that, "They rose from the tray like Mt. Everest.", which would lead the reader to believe they were piled really high.

36. B: Cranberry sauce was not served as part of the Thanksgiving dinner at the shelter.

37. D: The death of Chris's dad was the major problem the family had to deal with that eventually led to the their homelessness.

38. Part A: A: The author's intention in writing this piece is to persuade the reader to do something about homelessness.

Part B: D: Paragraph 1 does the best job of explaining why the author is writing this story.

39. B is the most complete and accurate summary of the story.

40. D is the best choice because the last paragraph of the story indicates that Ben is likely to serve at a homeless shelter again soon.

English Language Arts/Literacy Practice Test #2

Practice Questions

Questions 1 – 11 pertain to the following article:

The Trouble with Tests

(1) Lisa was a good student. She studied hard, diligently did her homework, and turned in assignments on time. Whenever she had to take a test, however, Lisa had a problem. Her hands began to sweat and her stomach began to churn. She felt dizzy and breathless and sick. As a result, Lisa couldn't focus and always did poorly on tests. Her grades suffered, and so did her confidence level.

(2) Lisa's problem is a common one. Often called test anxiety, it includes any unusual stress symptoms that occur during tests. Symptoms can be as mild as light nausea or headache, or as severe as vomiting or uncontrollable shaking. Millions of students deal with test anxiety every year, but few realize it can be improved through three simple steps.

(3) The first step to improving test anxiety is better study habits. Proper preparation is an important step to overcoming test anxiety. It is important to develop regular study times, avoiding last minute "cramming" for a test. Studying heavily on the day of or night before a test can actually increase test anxiety in most students. The better option is to devote at least a half-hour block of time to reviewing class materials each day. This can help embed information in the brain, making it more accessible at test time.

(4) Using memory games and tools is another way to improve study habits. Using these tools and games can help students better retain information. It also makes learning more fun, reducing stress levels. Flashcards with key points or ideas can be very helpful when used alone or with a study partner. Mnemonic devices—silly sayings to help students recall complex concepts—are also helpful tools for reducing stress and improving test performance. An example of a mnemonic device is "Every Good Boy Deserves Fudge" to help music students remember the note names for the lines of the treble clef staff (EGBDF).

(5) The second step to reducing test anxiety is to use relaxation techniques. The first relaxation technique that is useful for test anxiety is visualization. This involves choosing a favorite place or event. When test anxiety symptoms appear, students can close their eyes and visualize themselves in that favorite place or at that favorite event. The students should focus on sensory information—sights, sounds, smells, etc. This refocuses the attention of the brain and reduces anxiety.

(6) Another relaxation technique that works well for test anxiety is deep breathing. When the body is under stress, breathing becomes shallower, causing the heart rate to increase and the blood pressure to rise. Conscious deep breathing helps increase oxygen flow to the body, reducing the heart rate and blood pressure. To do deep

breathing, simply draw air in through the nose for five seconds, and then release the air through the mouth, blowing out steadily for five seconds. Done with eyes open or closed, deep breathing exercises reduce stress and relax the body.

(7) The third step to reducing test anxiety is positive self-talk. Often, test anxiety is the result of or is compounded by a lack of faith in abilities. Students can overcome this through positive self-talk and self-affirmation. Before each test, a student should repeat, "I can do this"—or some similar positive mantra—over and over. This can be done out loud or silently; either way, it creates a positive attitude and outlook that can reduce anxiety.

(8) The self-affirmation of celebrating success is a final key to overcoming test anxiety. Students should share test-taking victories with friends and loved ones. Students should also feel proud when they do well on a test. Every success is a blow to the obstacle of test anxiety. As with anything else, practice makes perfect, and celebrating success helps a student practice triumph over test anxiety.

(9) Test anxiety is a real problem, not an imagined issue or an excuse. It can be overcome, however, through three basic steps. First, students must use study tools and good habits for proper preparation. Second, students must use relaxation techniques—such as visualization and deep breathing—to help release stress from the body. Finally, students must engage in positive self-talk and celebrate successes to create an atmosphere of triumph. When all three of these steps are consistently practiced, test anxiety will become a thing of the past.

1. According to this article, what is test anxiety?

a. A hereditary psychological disease
b. Unusual stress symptoms that occur during tests
c. An allergy to stress that is triggered by tests
d. Headaches and nausea that occur after tests

2. What is a mnemonic device?

a. A silly saying used to help remember a complex concept
b. A tool that increases physical relaxation during a test
c. An old-fashioned torture device involving repeated testing
d. A tool for selecting answers on tests

3. What is the main purpose of this article?

a. To show that test anxiety is a common problem
b. To discuss Lisa's problems with test anxiety
c. To identify the symptoms of test anxiety
d. To identify potential solutions for test anxiety

4. What is the general tone of this article?

a. Entertaining
b. Persuasive
c. Informative
d. Fictional

5. Which of the following offers the best summary of this article?

a. Test anxiety is a common problem that can be improved through three simple steps
b. Lisa has test anxiety, and she needs to learn how to deal with it better
c. Relaxation techniques are the best method for preventing test anxiety
d. Good study habits are the best tools for preventing test anxiety

This question has two parts. Answer Part A, then answer Part B.
6. Part A: According to paragraph 3, what common study practice should be avoided?

a. Using flashcards
b. Studying with a partner
c. Last-minute studying
d. Over studying

Part B: What is another word used in the article to describe your answer in Part A?

a. filling
b. cramming
c. stuffing
d. overdoing

This question has two parts. Answer Part A, then answer Part B.

7. Part A: What is the first step to improving test anxiety?

a. Better study habits
b. Relaxation techniques
c. Self-affirmation and positive self-talk
d. Teamwork and study partners

Part B: Give a sentence from the paragraph that supports your answer in Part A.

____

____

____

8. Which of the following ideas is a supporting detail in this article?

a. Millions of students deal with test anxiety every year
b. Using memory games and tools improves study habits
c. Test anxiety is a real problem
d. "Every Good Boy Deserves Fudge" is an example of a study tool

9. What organizational pattern is used for this article?

a. Inverted pyramid
b. Proposition and support
c. Problem and solution
d. Simple exposition

10. What two specific relaxation techniques are discussed in this article?

a. Massage and deep breathing
b. Visualization and muscle tensing
c. Meditation and massage
d. Visualization and deep breathing

11. Which paragraph discusses the "final key" to overcoming test anxiety?

a. Paragraph 6
b. Paragraph 8
c. Paragraph 7
d. Paragraph 9

Questions 12-15 pertain to the following poem:

Fog

(1) Stealthy fog drifts through the air,
(2) A dense, gray blanket everywhere.
(3) It slowly seeps in from the sea,
(4) Clutching rooftops, climbing trees.
(5) Its eerie whisper fills the land—
(6) "Catch me, catch me, if you can!"
(7) It skims the sky and hugs the ground,
(8) Distorts the vision, muffles sound.
(9) It fills the mind and fools the feet
(10) Like haunting shadows in the street.
(11) It creeps across the alleyway
(12) And dims the newborn light of day.
(13) It smothers landscapes without shame
(14) Then fades as quickly as it came.

12. Which of the following is the best synonym for "stealthy"?

a. Evil
b. Careful
c. Sneaky
d. Thick

13. What type of figurative language is used in line 5?

a. Personification
b. Metaphor
c. Simile
d. Hyperbole

14. What does the poet accomplish by using figurative language throughout this poem?

a. The poet meets the basic requirements of poetry
b. The poet makes the fog seem alive
c. The poet confuses and overwhelms the reader
d. The poet gives additional length to the poem

15. To what is the fog compared in line 2?

a. A whisper
b. The sea
c. A shadow
d. A blanket

Questions 16– 20pertain to the following poem:

Summer Afternoon

(1) Golden sunlight bathes the meadow
(2) In brilliant midday glory.
(3) Slim green pillars bow in homage
(4) To a gentle summer breeze.
(5) Flowers turn their eager faces
(6) Upward to an azure sky.
(7) All is quiet, calm, and peaceful,
(8) Dozing in the pleasant heat.
(9) Just across the sleepy meadow
(10) A lazy stream meanders through,
(11) Sauntering between the banks
(12) Of hardened, sun-baked earth.
(13) Dragonflies flit to and fro
(14) Like scattered thoughts and fleeting dreams.
(15) Bright light glistens on the water
(16) Like sparkling, molten silver.
(17) The meadow rests in tacit glow
(18) As minutes turn to hours.
(19) The sun sinks lower in the sky,
(20) And shadows slowly lengthen.
(21) Daylight, dappled by the trees,
(22) Spreads across the open landscape
(23) Like a dim and dusky cloak,
(24) And—in silence—evening falls.

16. What do lines 3 and 4 refer to in a metaphor?

a. Green buildings in the field
b. Grasses waving in the wind
c. Trees waving in the wind
d. People worshipping the wind

17. What type of figurative language is used in lines 13 and 14?

a. Simile
b. Metaphor
c. Hyperbole
d. Personification

18. What does "tacit" mean in line 17?

a. Beautiful
b. Lazy
c. Silent
d. Bored

19. Which of the following best describes the mood of this poem?

a. Upbeat and exciting
b. Quiet and peaceful
c. Depressing and sullen
d. Happy and energetic

20. How many stanzas does this poem contain?

a. 1
b. 8
c. 3
d. 24

Questions 21 -22 pertain to both "Fog" and "Summer Afternoon":

This question has two parts. Answer Part A, then answer Part B.

21. Part A: What general theme is represented in both of these poems?

a. Nature
b. Water
c. Emotions
d. Time

Part B: Give an example from each poem that supports your answer from Part A.

____

____

____

____

22. What is the most important difference in the style of these two poems?

a. One uses figurative language and the other does not
b. One is longer than the other
c. One is set at night and the other is set in the daytime
d. One is rhymed and the other is free verse

Questions 23 – 30 pertain to the following story:

The Memory Quilt

(1) Kevin had been saving his allowance for months to buy a new bike. Now he was within a few dollars of his goal, and Grandma Ruth had offered to pay him to clean out her attic. Kevin was excited. The new bike was practically his!

(2) Early Saturday morning, Kevin's mom dropped him off at Grandma Ruth's house. Grandma Ruth hugged him. Then she walked upstairs with him and pointed him to a narrow ladder that led up to the attic.

(3) "It's a mess up there," she warned. "If you have any questions about anything, just ask. Most of it is old junk, though. You can sort things I won't want to keep into two piles—one to throw away and the other to donate to charity."

(4) Kevin climbed the ladder and looked around. Boxes and piles of old pictures and records and clothes littered the floor. It was a big job. He picked up a painting of flowers in a chipped wooden frame. It didn't look important, but Kevin thought he should check.

(5) "Grandma Ruth," he called, climbing down the ladder with the picture. "Is this important?"

(6) Grandma Ruth came out of her room and chuckled. "No, Kevin. Your grandfather and I bought that old picture at a yard sale years ago. Put it in the pile to donate to charity."

(7) Kevin climbed back up the ladder. He put the picture on the floor to start a pile for charity. Then he picked up an old, rusty toolbox. Like the old picture, it didn't look important, but Kevin thought he should check, just to make sure.

(8) "Grandma Ruth," he called again, climbing down the ladder with the toolbox. "Is this important?"

(9) Grandma Ruth laughed gently. "No, Kevin. Your grandfather bought that toolbox when we bought this old house. He was quite the handyman. But I have no use for it now. Put it in the pile to donate. And Kevin?"

(10) "Yes, Grandma Ruth?"

(11) "You don't have to check with me about each thing. If it looks old and unused, you can donate it or throw it away. I trust your judgment. But you can still ask if you have any questions." She winked at Kevin and went back into her room.

(12) Kevin climbed back up the ladder. He sorted through the piles quickly. By lunchtime, he was almost halfway done. He climbed down and ate tuna fish sandwiches with Grandma Ruth in the dining room. After lunch, she gave him some boxes to take up to the attic. She told him to box up and carry down the items to be donated to charity.

(13) Kevin made his way awkwardly back to the attic, carrying the boxes. He packed things up and sorted through piles until just before 4 pm, when his mom was coming to pick him up. The last item he grabbed was a faded, dusty quilt. He turned it over and studied it carefully. It was worn, and it seemed like it hadn't been used in a long time. Kevin threw it into a charity box and closed the top. Then he began carrying boxes down the ladder.

(14) Kevin's mom drove him by the Goodwill store on the way home. Together they unloaded the boxes of items to be donated. Then they headed home, where Kevin fell asleep right after dinner. He was exhausted from his hard work.

(15) Sunday afternoon, Kevin went back to Grandma Ruth's house to finish cleaning out the attic. The piles were sparser now, but they still popped up from the dusty floor like wayward molehills. He got right to work, sorting, boxing things up, and neatly stacking the items to be kept.

(16) Halfway through the afternoon, Grandma Ruth called Kevin down for cookies and milk.

(17) "Kevin, have you seen my old patchwork quilt up in the attic?" Grandma Ruth asked. "I can't seem to find it anywhere. I made that quilt from your grandfather's old work shirts and your mom's first baby blanket and the tablecloth I got at my wedding. There are so many memories in that quilt."

(18) Kevin gulped. He didn't want to lie to Grandma Ruth, but he couldn't tell her he donated her precious quilt to charity. She would kill him!

(19) "I'll look for it when I go back up," he promised, knowing it wasn't there.

(20) At the end of the afternoon, Kevin was done cleaning the attic. He carried the last box down the ladder.

(21) "Did you see my quilt up there?" Grandma Ruth asked.

(22) "No," Kevin said, half-truthfully.

(23) "I wonder where it could be," Grandma Ruth said.

(24) When Kevin and his mom stopped at the Goodwill store to donate the last set of boxes, Kevin asked if he could run inside. He dashed in and browsed the shelves carefully. Then he saw it. It was stuffed between two stacks of throw pillows. It was almost hidden, but unmistakable. He pulled out the quilt and checked the price.

(25) Kevin's heart fell. Paying for the quilt would mean he would have to wait another month or two to buy his bike. If he just went home, no one would ever know about his mistake. But he knew that would be wrong. Buying the quilt back was the right thing to do. Kevin paid for the quilt and hurried back to the car.

(26) Kevin's mom looked at the quilt with surprise. "Isn't that Grandma Ruth's memory quilt?"

(27) Kevin nodded glumly. He told his mom the whole story. Then he said he needed to go back to Grandma Ruth's house to tell her the truth.

(28) "I'm proud of you," Kevin's mom said as she turned the car around. "Let's go give Grandma Ruth back her memories."

23. What is the primary setting for this story?

a. Grandma Ruth's attic
b. The Goodwill store
c. Kevin's house
d. Grandma Ruth's dining room

This question has two parts. Answer Part A, then answer Part B.

24. Part A: In paragraph 15, what does "sparser" mean?

a. Denser
b. Larger and higher
c. Fewer and smaller
d. More organized

Part B: Which of the following is an antonym for "sparser"?

a. spacious
b. petite
c. barren
d. abundant

25. What point of view is used to tell this story?

a. First person
b. Second person
c. Third person
d. All of the above

26. What type of figurative language is used in paragraph 15?

a. Metaphor
b. Personification
c. Hyperbole
d. Simile

27. What is the general theme of this story?

a. Help your grandmother
b. Cleaning is best done in an organized way
c. Do the right thing
d. Never throw away or donate old items

28. Why was the quilt so valuable to Grandma Ruth?

a. It contained fabric from memorable things
b. It was sewn by hand by her grandmother
c. She had used the quilt for many years
d. It was a wedding present from Kevin's grandfather

29. Which of the following is a supporting detail in this story?

a. Kevin was saving his allowance for a new bike
b. Kevin and Grandma Ruth ate tuna fish sandwiches
c. Kevin was cleaning out Grandma Ruth's attic
d. Kevin donated Grandma Ruth's quilt to charity

30. Write a brief summary of this story?

____

____

____

Questions 31 – 40 pertain to the following article:

Like Riding a Kite

(1) Imagine soaring high above the earth. There is no engine, no fuselage beneath you. There is only you, your glider, the wind, and the sky. It's like riding a kite with no strings attached, rising and falling on the breeze like a bird. It is freedom and thrill and ultimate pleasure. This is the world of hang gliding.

(2) While many people have a general idea of what hang gliding is all about, few really understand the sport. Most people don't realize a majestic glider can be collapsed to the size of a duffel bag. Few people know that gliders can stay aloft for hours and that the world distance record for a single glider flight is nearly 190 miles. Even fewer people realize that a hang glider can actually climb in the sky, even without an engine. In California, in the 1980s, one expert glider pilot gained more than 14,000 feet of altitude after takeoff! Hang gliders have mind-boggling capabilities.

(3) The amazing sport of hang gliding has a rich history dating back to the 1890s. In 1891, the first hang glider was invented by Otto Lilienthal in Germany. It was made of wood and cloth, weighed 40 pounds, was 23 feet wide, and could go about 35 miles per hour (mph) at an altitude of 100 feet. British inventor Percy Picher also built gliders with similar features in the late 1890s. Unfortunately, both inventors were killed in glider crashes before their designs were perfected. With the element of danger involved in early hang gliding—and with the advent of airplane flight by the Wright brothers in 1903—many people lost interest in hang gliding.

(4) After the end of World War II, however, many military-trained pilots wanted to keep flying. Airplanes were too expensive for most people, so the sport of hang gliding was reborn. Through invention and innovation, new designs for hang gliders began to emerge. These included new materials and designs for glider construction and the addition of a control bar to improve safety. The basic design for today's hang gliders premiered at a meet in California in 1971. It included a broad, flexible wing on a sturdy frame with a control bar and a seat or safety harness.

(5) Since 1971, few major design changes have been made to hang gliders, although as new materials for construction become available, minor changes are made to improve flight. Modern sails range from 13 to 28 feet across. They are made of durable, lightweight, manmade fabric—such as nylon—and are designed to flex in shape and tension based on the wind. The sail is attached to a frame made from aluminum tubing. The frame includes a control bar, shaped like a rounded triangle and used for steering. Suspended from the frame is a harness or seat to improve pilot comfort and safety.

(6) Another way pilots improve comfort and safety is through the use of proper gear and equipment. Pilots should wear light, protective clothing and gloves designed for hang gliding. A helmet is also an important safety component. In addition, pilots need special instruments that are used during flight. These tools help measure thermals, the warm air currents used to lift and propel gliders through the air.

(7) Thermals are important to both taking off and staying aloft, but they aren't the only factor in flight. Modern gliders weigh about 35 pounds and are special balanced to a pilot's weight and preferences. To take off, the pilot is secured in the glider and then runs off the edge of a large hill or cliff, where thermals catch the glider and lift it into the air. If the wind is sustained at 12 mph or above, the pilot may even be able to take off without running. Once the glider is airborne, the pilot steers by shifting his/her weight and using the control bar. Each glider has its own unique feel, and a pilot must know the glider well to achieve a safe takeoff, flight, and landing.

(8) In addition to knowing the unique feel of the glider, a pilot must know the safety rules of the sky to have a safe flight. Pilots of hang gliders do not need to be licensed, but they must obey all rules and laws for flying. Hang glider pilots should never fly in bad weather or high winds. They must yield the right of way to any aircraft in distress and all hot air balloons. They must never intentionally fly into a cloud or a flock of birds. Finally, hang glider pilots should stay at least five miles away from airports during flight and at least 100 feet from buildings, telephone wires and poles, populated places, and crowds.

(9) Throughout history, mankind has looked for a way to soar with the birds across the canvas of the sky. Hang gliding offers that opportunity. With modern features and equipment, and with proper training in techniques and the rules of the sky, hang glider pilots can safely experience the thrill of flight. In a glider, the pilot is one with the breeze, the sunlight, the world itself. Hang gliding is truly like riding a kite through the expanse of the heavens.

31. In paragraph 3, what does "advent" mean?

a. End
b. Beginning
c. Expansion
d. Popularity

32. Which of the following is the best definition of "thermals" as it is used in this article?

a. Protective clothing for pilots
b. Aluminum tubing used in glider frames
c. Tools used by pilots for safety
d. Warm air currents that lift gliders

33. What was the author's main purpose in writing this article?

a. To inform
b. To entertain
c. To analyze
d. To persuade

34. What type of figurative language is used in the first sentence of paragraph 9?

a. No figurative language is used in the first sentence of paragraph 9
b. Simile
c. Metaphor
d. Hyperbole

35. From what point of view is this article written?

a. First person
b. Second person
c. Third person
d. All of the above

36. Which of the following best describes the theme of this article?

a. Hang gliding has a rich history that began in the 1890s with two inventors
b. Modern hang gliding has come far and is a safe, fun way to soar through the sky
c. Hang gliders are 13 to 28 feet wide and have a sturdy frame and harness or seat
d. The modern hang glider premiered at a meet in California in 1971

37. What material is used to make modern hang glider frames?

a. Aluminum
b. Steel
c. Wood
d. PVC

38. Who invented the first hang glider in 1891?

a. Percy Picher
b. The Wright brothers
c. Donald Regalo
d. Otto Lilienthal

This question has two parts. Answer Part A, then answer Part B.

39. Part A: Which of the following is a main idea in this article?

a. Modern glider sails are 13 to 28 feet wide
b. Glider pilots must know the rules of the sky
c. All glider pilots should wear helmets for safety
d. Modern glider design premiered in 1971

Part B: Give a supporting detail that supports your answer in Part A.

____

____

____

40. How did World War II positively impact the sport of hang gliding?

a. It did not positively impact the sport of hang gliding
b. Gliders were used in World War II in Europe and Asia
c. Returning military pilots wanted to fly but couldn't afford planes
d. Flight had become much safer due to World War II technology

Answers and Explanations

1. B: In paragraph 1, we learn that Lisa does poorly on tests because she suffers from a variety of unusual symptoms whenever she takes a test. In paragraph 2, the author tells us that there's a name for this condition, which is test anxiety.

2. A: The explanation of a mnemonic device is found in paragraph 4.

3. D: The main purpose of this article is to identify potential solutions for test anxiety. The passage starts out by describing what test anxiety is, and then goes on to explain three ways to overcome it.

4. C: The tone of this article is informative. It's not fictional, and it's not trying to entertain readers, or persuade them to do something. It simply gives people information about what test anxiety is, and what they can do about it if they suffer from it.

5. A: This answer choice offers the best summary of the article.

6. Part A: C: According to paragraph 3, last-minute studying should be avoided.

Part B: B: It paragraph 3 it states you should avoid "last minute "cramming" for a test".

7. Part A: We learn in paragraph 3 that the first step to reducing test anxiety is better study habits.

Part B: There are several sentences that will support your answer. "Proper preparation is an important step to overcoming test anxiety." or " It is important to develop regular study times, avoiding last minute "cramming" for a test.

8. D: This is the only answer choice that is a supporting detail. In other words, it represents a minor point of the article. A, B, and C are incorrect because they all represent main ideas in the article, not supporting details.

9. C: This article is organized in a problem-and-solution format.

10. D: Two specific relaxation techniques mentioned in the article are visualization and deep breathing. They can be found in paragraphs 5 and 6.

11. B: Paragraph 8 discusses the "final key" to overcoming test anxiety.

12. C: The word *sneaky* has almost the same meaning as *stealthy,* which means "quietly and secretly." When someone is doing something stealthily, they are trying to do something without been seen or heard.

13. A: Personification is using language that attributes human characteristics to non-human things. Line 5 uses personification when it suggests that the fog has an "eerie whisper."

14. B: The poet has filled this poem with figurative language to give the reader the impression that the fog is a living, breathing, thinking creature.

15. D: In line 2, the fog is compared to a "dense, gray blanket."

16. B: The metaphor in lines 3 and 4 refers to grasses waving in the wind.

17. A: Lines 13 and 14 contain a simile comparing the dragonflies to "scattered thoughts and fleeting dreams."

18. C: In line 17, "tacit" means silent.

19. B: The mood of this poem is quiet and peaceful. The author creates this mood by carefully choosing words, phrases, and rhythms to bring about these feelings in the reader.

20. C: This poem contains 3 stanzas. A stanza is a lot of sentences grouped together. In a poem, a stanza functions like a paragraph does in a prose piece.

21. Part A: A: Even though the poems are about two different subjects, fog and a summer afternoon, the general theme of both poems is nature.

Part B: The first poem is about fog so a good example is "Stealthy fog drifts through the air," The second poem is about summer so a good example would be "Golden sunlight bathes the meadow"

22. D: The most important difference between the styles of these two poems is that one is rhymed and the other is free verse.

23. A: Some scenes take place in other places, but the main setting for this story is Grandma Ruth's attic, because that's where the bulk of the story actually takes place.

24. Part A: C: The phrase "fewer and smaller" is a good definition for "sparser" as it is used in paragraph 15. Kevin could see that he was making progress because there were fewer piles of junk left, and the ones that remained were smaller than they had been.
Part B: D: "abundant" is the best choice because its means there is large amount.

25. C: This story is written in third-person point of view. That means it's being told about the characters in the story, not by any of them. If it had been written as if Kevin or his grandmother were telling the story, it would be in the first-person.

26. D: In paragraph 15 the piles of junk are compared to mole hills using "like," making the comparison a simile.

27. C: The general theme of this story is "do the right thing." Even though it will cost Kevin some money, and it will mean that he will have to go without a new bike for several more weeks, he goes back to the store and purchases the quilt that meant so much to his grandmother.

28. A: In paragraph 17, Grandma Ruth tells Kevin that the quilt held so many important memories for her.

29. B: This answer choice is the only one that is a supporting detail. The fact that they had tuna sandwiches for lunch doesn't mean much to the overall story. The other answer choices represent things that are important to the development of the story.

30. B: A good summary would be something like: While cleaning out Grandma Ruth's attic, Kevin donates an important quilt to charity and has to get it back.

31. B: The word *advent* means "beginning."

32. D: is the best choice because in this article, *thermals* are warm air currents that lift gliders. The definition of the word can be found in paragraph 6: "These tools help measure thermals, the warm air currents used to lift and propel gliders through the air."

33. A: The author's main purpose in writing this article is to tell the reader about hang gliding – how long it's been taking place, how it got started, how it works, some rules and safety guidelines, etc.

34. C: The first sentence of paragraph 9 uses a metaphor to compare the sky to a canvas.

35. C: This article is written in third-person point of view. If the author were talking about his own experiences, using words such as *I* and *me*, then it would be in the first-person.

36. B: is the best choice because it offers the most accurate description of the theme of the article. A, C, and D are all points mentioned in the passage, but they do not accurately and completely describe the theme of the article.

37. A: Modern hang glider frames are made from aluminum. This information can be found in paragraph 5.

38. D: Paragraph 3 says that Otto Lilienthal invented the first hang glider in 1891.

39. Part A: B: This is the only option that represents a main idea of the article. A, C, and D are not the best choices because they are all supporting details, not main ideas of the article.

Part B: In the passage it states "a pilot must know the safety rules of the sky to have a safe flight."

40. C: Paragraph 4 says that hang gliding experienced a revival of interest after World War II, when many military pilots were frustrated after coming home from the war, because they couldn't afford to fly planes, so they took up hang gliding.

How to Overcome Test Anxiety

Just the thought of taking a test is enough to make most people a little nervous. A test is an important event that can have a long-term impact on your future, so it's important to take it seriously and it's natural to feel anxious about performing well. But just because anxiety is normal, that doesn't mean that it's helpful in test taking, or that you should simply accept it as part of your life. Anxiety can have a variety of effects. These effects can be mild, like making you feel slightly nervous, or severe, like blocking your ability to focus or remember even a simple detail.

If you experience test anxiety—whether severe or mild—it's important to know how to beat it. To discover this, first you need to understand what causes test anxiety.

Causes of Test Anxiety

While we often think of anxiety as an uncontrollable emotional state, it can actually be caused by simple, practical things. One of the most common causes of test anxiety is that a person does not feel adequately prepared for their test. This feeling can be the result of many different issues such as poor study habits or lack of organization, but the most common culprit is time management. Starting to study too late, failing to organize your study time to cover all of the material, or being distracted while you study will mean that you're not well prepared for the test. This may lead to cramming the night before, which will cause you to be physically and mentally exhausted for the test. Poor time management also contributes to feelings of stress, fear, and hopelessness as you realize you are not well prepared but don't know what to do about it.

Other times, test anxiety is not related to your preparation for the test but comes from unresolved fear. This may be a past failure on a test, or poor performance on tests in general. It may come from comparing yourself to others who seem to be performing better or from the stress of living up to expectations. Anxiety may be driven by fears of the future—how failure on this test would affect your educational and career goals. These fears are often completely irrational, but they can still negatively impact your test performance.

Elements of Test Anxiety

As mentioned earlier, test anxiety is considered to be an emotional state, but it has physical and mental components as well. Sometimes you may not even realize that you are suffering from test anxiety until you notice the physical symptoms. These can include trembling hands, rapid heartbeat, sweating, nausea, and tense muscles. Extreme anxiety may lead to fainting or vomiting. Obviously, any of these symptoms can have a negative impact on testing. It is important to recognize them as soon as they begin to occur so that you can address the problem before it damages your performance.

The mental components of test anxiety include trouble focusing and inability to remember learned information. During a test, your mind is on high alert, which can help you recall information and stay focused for an extended period of time. However, anxiety interferes with your mind's natural processes, causing you to blank out, even on the questions you know well. The strain of testing during anxiety makes it difficult to stay focused, especially on a test that may take several hours. Extreme anxiety can take a huge mental toll, making it difficult not only to recall test information but even to understand the test questions or pull your thoughts together.

Effects of Test Anxiety

Test anxiety is like a disease—if left untreated, it will get progressively worse. Anxiety leads to poor performance, and this reinforces the feelings of fear and failure, which in turn lead to poor performances on subsequent tests. It can grow from a mild nervousness to a crippling condition. If allowed to progress, test anxiety can have a big impact on your schooling, and consequently on your future.

Test anxiety can spread to other parts of your life. Anxiety on tests can become anxiety in any stressful situation, and blanking on a test can turn into panicking in a job situation. But fortunately, you don't have to let anxiety rule your testing and determine your grades. There are a number of relatively simple steps you can take to move past anxiety and function normally on a test and in the rest of life.

Physical Steps for Beating Test Anxiety

While test anxiety is a serious problem, the good news is that it can be overcome. It doesn't have to control your ability to think and remember information. While it may take time, you can begin taking steps today to beat anxiety.

Just as your first hint that you may be struggling with anxiety comes from the physical symptoms, the first step to treating it is also physical. Rest is crucial for having a clear, strong mind. If you are tired, it is much easier to give in to anxiety. But if you establish good sleep habits, your body and mind will be ready to perform optimally, without the strain of exhaustion. Additionally, sleeping well helps you to retain information better, so you're more likely to recall the answers when you see the test questions.

Getting good sleep means more than going to bed on time. It's important to allow your brain time to relax. Take study breaks from time to time so it doesn't get overworked, and don't study right before bed. Take time to rest your mind before trying to rest your body, or you may find it difficult to fall asleep.

Along with sleep, other aspects of physical health are important in preparing for a test. Good nutrition is vital for good brain function. Sugary foods and drinks may give a burst of energy but this burst is followed by a crash, both physically and emotionally. Instead, fuel your body with protein and vitamin-rich foods.

Also, drink plenty of water. Dehydration can lead to headaches and exhaustion, especially if your brain is already under stress from the rigors of the test. Particularly if your test is a long one, drink water during the breaks. And if possible, take an energy-boosting snack to eat between sections.

Along with sleep and diet, a third important part of physical health is exercise. Maintaining a steady workout schedule is helpful, but even taking 5-minute study breaks to walk can help get your blood pumping faster and clear your head. Exercise also releases endorphins, which contribute to a positive feeling and can help combat test anxiety.

When you nurture your physical health, you are also contributing to your mental health. If your body is healthy, your mind is much more likely to be healthy as well. So take time to rest, nourish your body with healthy food and water, and get moving as much as possible. Taking these physical steps will make you stronger and more able to take the mental steps necessary to overcome test anxiety.

Mental Steps for Beating Test Anxiety

Working on the mental side of test anxiety can be more challenging, but as with the physical side, there are clear steps you can take to overcome it. As mentioned earlier, test anxiety often stems from lack of preparation, so the obvious solution is to prepare for the test. Effective studying may be the most important weapon you have for beating test anxiety, but you can and should employ several other mental tools to combat fear.

First, boost your confidence by reminding yourself of past success—tests or projects that you aced. If you're putting as much effort into preparing for this test as you did for those, there's no reason you should expect to fail here. Work hard to prepare; then trust your preparation.

Second, surround yourself with encouraging people. It can be helpful to find a study group, but be sure that the people you're around will encourage a positive attitude. If you spend time with others who are anxious or cynical, this will only contribute to your own anxiety. Look for others who are motivated to study hard from a desire to succeed, not from a fear of failure.

Third, reward yourself. A test is physically and mentally tiring, even without anxiety, and it can be helpful to have something to look forward to. Plan an activity following the test, regardless of the outcome, such as going to a movie or getting ice cream.

When you are taking the test, if you find yourself beginning to feel anxious, remind yourself that you know the material. Visualize successfully completing the test. Then take a few deep, relaxing breaths and return to it. Work through the questions carefully but with confidence, knowing that you are capable of succeeding.

Developing a healthy mental approach to test taking will also aid in other areas of life. Test anxiety affects more than just the actual test—it can be damaging to your mental health and even contribute to depression. It's important to beat test anxiety before it becomes a problem for more than testing.

Study Strategy

Being prepared for the test is necessary to combat anxiety, but what does being prepared look like? You may study for hours on end and still not feel prepared. What you need is a strategy for test prep. The next few pages outline our recommended steps to help you plan out and conquer the challenge of preparation.

Step 1: Scope Out the Test

Learn everything you can about the format (multiple choice, essay, etc.) and what will be on the test. Gather any study materials, course outlines, or sample exams that may be available. Not only will this help you to prepare, but knowing what to expect can help to alleviate test anxiety.

Step 2: Map Out the Material

Look through the textbook or study guide and make note of how many chapters or sections it has. Then divide these over the time you have. For example, if a book has 15 chapters and you have five days to study, you need to cover three chapters each day. Even better, if you have the time, leave an extra day at the end for overall review after you have gone through the material in depth.

If time is limited, you may need to prioritize the material. Look through it and make note of which sections you think you already have a good grasp on, and which need review. While you are studying, skim quickly through the familiar sections and take more time on the challenging parts.

Write out your plan so you don't get lost as you go. Having a written plan also helps you feel more in control of the study, so anxiety is less likely to arise from feeling overwhelmed at the amount to cover.

Step 3: Gather Your Tools

Decide what study method works best for you. Do you prefer to highlight in the book as you study and then go back over the highlighted portions? Or do you type out notes of the important information? Or is it helpful to make flashcards that you can carry with you? Assemble the pens, index cards, highlighters, post-it notes, and any other materials you may need so you won't be distracted by getting up to find things while you study.

If you're having a hard time retaining the information or organizing your notes, experiment with different methods. For example, try color-coding by subject with colored pens, highlighters, or post-it notes. If you learn better by hearing, try recording yourself reading your notes so you can listen while in the car, working out, or simply sitting at your desk. Ask a friend to quiz you from your flashcards, or try teaching someone the material to solidify it in your mind.

Step 4: Create Your Environment

It's important to avoid distractions while you study. This includes both the obvious distractions like visitors and the subtle distractions like an uncomfortable chair (or a too-comfortable couch that makes you want to fall asleep). Set up the best study environment possible: good lighting and a comfortable work area. If background music helps you focus, you may want to turn it on, but otherwise keep the room quiet. If you are using a computer to take notes, be sure you don't have any other windows open, especially applications like social media, games, or anything else that could distract you. Silence your phone and turn off notifications. Be sure to keep water close by so you stay hydrated while you study (but avoid unhealthy drinks and snacks).

Also, take into account the best time of day to study. Are you freshest first thing in the morning? Try to set aside some time then to work through the material. Is your mind clearer in the afternoon or evening? Schedule your study session then. Another method is to study at the same time of day that you will take the test, so that your brain gets used to working on the material at that time and will be ready to focus at test time.

Step 5: Study!

Once you have done all the study preparation, it's time to settle into the actual studying. Sit down, take a few moments to settle your mind so you can focus, and begin to follow your study plan. Don't give in to distractions or let yourself procrastinate. This is your time to prepare so you'll be ready to fearlessly approach the test. Make the most of the time and stay focused.

Of course, you don't want to burn out. If you study too long you may find that you're not retaining the information very well. Take regular study breaks. For example, taking five minutes out of every hour to walk briskly, breathing deeply and swinging your arms, can help your mind stay fresh.

As you get to the end of each chapter or section, it's a good idea to do a quick review. Remind yourself of what you learned and work on any difficult parts. When you feel that you've mastered the material, move on to the next part. At the end of your study session, briefly skim through your notes again.

But while review is helpful, cramming last minute is NOT. If at all possible, work ahead so that you won't need to fit all your study into the last day. Cramming overloads your brain with more information than it can process and retain, and your tired mind may struggle to recall even previously learned information when it is overwhelmed with last-minute study. Also, the urgent nature of cramming and the stress placed on your brain contribute to anxiety. You'll be more likely to go to the test feeling unprepared and having trouble thinking clearly.

So don't cram, and don't stay up late before the test, even just to review your notes at a leisurely pace. Your brain needs rest more than it needs to go over the information again. In fact, plan to finish your studies by noon or early afternoon the day before the test. Give your brain the rest of the day to relax or focus on other things, and get a good night's sleep. Then you will be fresh for the test and better able to recall what you've studied.

Step 6: Take a Practice Test

Many courses offer sample tests, either online or in the study materials. This is an excellent resource to check whether you have mastered the material, as well as to prepare for the test format and environment.

Check the test format ahead of time: the number of questions, the type (multiple choice, free response, etc.), and the time limit. Then create a plan for working through them. For example, if you have 30 minutes to take a 60-question test, your limit is 30 seconds per question. Spend less time on the questions you know well so that you can take more time on the difficult ones.

If you have time to take several practice tests, take the first one open book, with no time limit. Work through the questions at your own pace and make sure you fully understand them. Gradually work up to taking a test under test conditions: sit at a desk with all study materials put away and set a timer. Pace yourself to make sure you finish the test with time to spare and go back to check your answers if you have time.

After each test, check your answers. On the questions you missed, be sure you understand why you missed them. Did you misread the question (tests can use tricky wording)? Did you forget the information? Or was it something you hadn't learned? Go back and study any shaky areas that the practice tests reveal.

Taking these tests not only helps with your grade, but also aids in combating test anxiety. If you're already used to the test conditions, you're less likely to worry about it, and working through tests until you're scoring well gives you a confidence boost. Go through the practice tests until you feel comfortable, and then you can go into the test knowing that you're ready for it.

Test Tips

On test day, you should be confident, knowing that you've prepared well and are ready to answer the questions. But aside from preparation, there are several test day strategies you can employ to maximize your performance.

First, as stated before, get a good night's sleep the night before the test (and for several nights before that, if possible). Go into the test with a fresh, alert mind rather than staying up late to study.

Try not to change too much about your normal routine on the day of the test. It's important to eat a nutritious breakfast, but if you normally don't eat breakfast at all, consider eating just a protein bar. If you're a coffee drinker, go ahead and have your normal coffee. Just make sure you time it so that the caffeine doesn't wear off right in the middle of your test. Avoid sugary beverages, and drink enough water to stay hydrated but not so much that you need a restroom break 10 minutes into the test. If your test isn't first thing in the morning, consider going for a walk or doing a light workout before the test to get your blood flowing.

Allow yourself enough time to get ready, and leave for the test with plenty of time to spare so you won't have the anxiety of scrambling to arrive in time. Another reason to be early is to select a good seat. It's helpful to sit away from doors and windows, which can be distracting. Find a good seat, get out your supplies, and settle your mind before the test begins.

When the test begins, start by going over the instructions carefully, even if you already know what to expect. Make sure you avoid any careless mistakes by following the directions.

Then begin working through the questions, pacing yourself as you've practiced. If you're not sure on an answer, don't spend too much time on it, and don't let it shake your confidence. Either skip it and come back later, or eliminate as many wrong answers as possible and guess among the remaining ones. Don't dwell on these questions as you continue—put them out of your mind and focus on what lies ahead.

Be sure to read all of the answer choices, even if you're sure the first one is the right answer. Sometimes you'll find a better one if you keep reading. But don't second-guess yourself if you do immediately know the answer. Your gut instinct is usually right. Don't let test anxiety rob you of the information you know.

If you have time at the end of the test (and if the test format allows), go back and review your answers. Be cautious about changing any, since your first instinct tends to be correct, but make sure you didn't misread any of the questions or accidentally mark the wrong answer choice. Look over any you skipped and make an educated guess.

At the end, leave the test feeling confident. You've done your best, so don't waste time worrying about your performance or wishing you could change anything. Instead, celebrate the successful completion of this test. And finally, use this test to learn how to deal with anxiety even better next time.

Review Video: Test Anxiety
Visit mometrix.com/academy and enter code: 100340

Important Qualification

Not all anxiety is created equal. If your test anxiety is causing major issues in your life beyond the classroom or testing center, or if you are experiencing troubling physical symptoms related to your anxiety, it may be a sign of a serious physiological or psychological condition. If this sounds like your situation, we strongly encourage you to seek professional help.

Thank You

We at Mometrix would like to extend our heartfelt thanks to you, our friend and patron, for allowing us to play a part in your journey. It is a privilege to serve people from all walks of life who are unified in their commitment to building the best future they can for themselves.

The preparation you devote to these important testing milestones may be the most valuable educational opportunity you have for making a real difference in your life. We encourage you to put your heart into it—that feeling of succeeding, overcoming, and yes, conquering will be well worth the hours you've invested.

We want to hear your story, your struggles and your successes, and if you see any opportunities for us to improve our materials so we can help others even more effectively in the future, please share that with us as well. **The team at Mometrix would be absolutely thrilled to hear from you!** So please, send us an email (support@mometrix.com) and let's stay in touch.

If you'd like some additional help, check out these other resources we offer for your exam: http://MometrixFlashcards.com/CCSS

Online Resources

Due to our efforts to try to keep this book to a manageable length, we've created a link that will give you access to all of your online resources:

mometrix.com/resources719/ccg6ela

It's Your Moment, Let's Celebrate It!

Share your story @mometrixtestpreparation